MICHEL ROUX
Cheese

MICHEL ROUX
Cheese

THE ESSENTIAL GUIDE TO COOKING
WITH CHEESE, OVER 100 RECIPES

Contents

Notes

All spoon measures are level unless otherwise stated: 1 tsp = 5ml spoon; 1 tbsp = 15ml spoon.

Use fresh herbs, sea salt and freshly ground black pepper unless otherwise suggested.

If using the zest of citrus fruit, buy organic, unwaxed fruit.

Timings are for conventional ovens. If using a fan-assisted oven, lower the temperature by 15°C. Use an oven thermometer to check the temperature.

Introduction

The numerous journeys I made through France while I was writing my last book, *The Essence of French Cooking*, rekindled many childhood memories for me, including, among others, my discovery and love of cheese... so much so, in fact, that I decided to devote my next book to the subject.

From the age of seven, my mother entrusted me with the task of buying a few items from the local market of St Mandé every Thursday. I would set off around midday to arrive when the stallholders were reducing their prices, preferring to sell their wares for less rather than having to pack everything up again. After buying fruit and vegetables, and some meat or fish, I was drawn like a magnet towards the cheese stall. The pleasure for me, as a kid, was an awakening of all my senses: smell, sight, touch and taste.

Every market day was invariably a voyage of discovery for me, because new cheeses appeared on the stall in different shapes, sizes and colours with the changing season, only to disappear again after a few months... I used to think that they wanted to play hide-and-seek with me. The woman on the stall would always spoil me. I think she loved seeing my face light up in front of the display of cheeses, my eyes devouring them all. She would give me little morsels to try, especially the fresh cheeses or any that were relatively mild on the palate while still being flavourful. Through her gentle handling, she succeeded in developing my palate.

Our finances didn't allow us to spend a fortune on cheese, and my mother's instructions were strict: I must use the few precious coins deep in my pocket to get maximum value for money. I would often pick Cantal, a cheese known at the time as 'poor man's cheese', since it was the least expensive, yet nourishing, or a piece of Gruyère that, according to my mother, was vital for bone growth. Sometimes I'd choose a Camembert or half a Coulommiers, first checking it was perfectly ripe to the centre by pressing it with my thumb. A piece of Roquefort, the king of cheeses, was a real treat. It was expensive, so I would buy just a tiny piece – around 50g – to spread over a whole baguette to pass around the table and share on a Sunday.

So there you have it, that is how I discovered my love of cheese. Since then, of course, I have come across hundreds of types of cheese on my extensive travels around the world. And at our restaurant the Waterside Inn, we offer our clients a choice of between 30 and 40 cheeses every day.

Cheese-making

It is thought that the first cheeses were made accidentally, thousands of years ago, as a consequence of herdsman carrying milk in leather bottles. Rennet, an enzyme found in a calf's stomach, curdled the milk in the bottle, creating the earliest cheese. Over the centuries the process has, of course, been much refined, but it is still based on a simple technique, involving four basic ingredients: milk, a starter culture, rennet (or other curdling agent) and salt.

Cow's milk is most commonly used, but cheese-makers also produce cheeses from goat's, sheep's and buffalo milk. Of the dozen or so dairy cattle breeds, the Holstein-Friesian is the most widespread. Dairy cows produce around 25 litres of milk a day each, and Germany is the biggest producer of cow's milk in Europe.

France is the largest producer and consumer of goat's cheese in Europe. Of the goat milking breeds, the Saanen is the best known. One goat produces between 2 and 5 litres a day, depending on the actual breed and its environs.

Sheep's or ewe's milk is naturally homogenised and richer in fat and protein than cow's milk, making it ideal for cheese-making. One ewe produces around 1 litre of milk per day. The Lacaune breed is the most popular in France, which produces a wide variety of ewe's cheeses, including the famous Roquefort. Greece, Italy and Spain also produce excellent cheeses from sheep's milk.

Buffalo milk, from water buffalo, is primarily used to produce mozzarella. Italy is the main producer, of course, but good mozzarella is also produced in other countries around the world.

Whichever type of milk is used, the cheese-making process is similar. Firstly, a bacterial culture is added to the milk to acidify it. The bacteria turn the lactose in the milk to lactic acid, effectively souring it. Rennet or a non-animal curdling agent is then added to coagulate the milk, turning it into curds (the solid part) and whey (the liquid). The curds, which will become the cheese, are left to set and separate from the whey. This first stage forms the basis of the cheese.

The exact procedures during the subsequent stages determine the type or 'category' of cheese. With the exception of most of the fresh cheeses (see right), the second stage involves concentrating the curd. Firstly, to release the whey, the curds are cut – lightly for soft cheeses or finely for hard cheeses. After this, the curds are either 'cooked' or piled on top of each other and pressed to exclude more whey. The curd is then milled and salt is added.

The third and final stage is the ripening process, during which the flavour and texture of the cheese develops. This is achieved by storing the cheese for a certain length of time in an area where the temperature and humidity are controlled. The type of cheese determines the precise conditions and length of storage, which account for its individual characteristics.

Cheese categories

Broadly, all cheeses belong to one of the following categories, according to the way they are produced:

   Fresh cheeses These moist, young cheeses are ready to eat plain, just as they are, a few hours after being made. The curds are not cut, pressed or ripened (except for feta), so they represent the first stage of a cheese. Gently flavoured and low in fat, these milky cheeses are very mild and creamy, with just a hint of acidity. Ricotta, mozzarella and feta fall into this category, and there are many fresh goat's cheeses.
   Soft cheeses with a natural rind Often made in small log or pyramid shapes, these cheeses have a relatively fine rind covered in a light whitish to grey mould. They are mainly made from goat's or sheep's milk and tend to have a creamy texture and mild flavour. In fact, they are fresh cheeses that are left to age and dry out, often in temperature- and humidity-controlled caves, reaching maturity after 10 to 30 days. Fine examples include Sainte-Maure de Touraine, Crottin de Chavignol and Valençay.
   Soft cheeses with a bloomy rind Made with cow's, goat's or sheep's milk, these are surface-ripened and have a white rind casing. The flavour of these cheeses ranges from very mild (sometimes with light mushroomy and almond aromas), to fairly strong, and their texture from slightly granular to runny. My favourites are Normandy Camembert, Brillat-Savarin and Sharpham Brie.
   Soft cheeses with a washed rind These cheeses are immersed in brine in various ways, which produces a relatively thin firm rind, ranging from yellow to orange. The brine curing gives their flavour more character too, resulting in fairly pronounced notes. Washed-rind cheeses also often undergo a slow ripening stage, which gives them a more distinctive and supple texture. Cheeses in this category include Vacherin Mont d'Or, Saint-Nectaire, Langres and Stinking Bishop.
   Semi-hard cheeses As the name implies, these have a texture somewhere between soft and hard cheeses. These cheeses are pressed in moulds after the curd has been cut and 'piled'. They are usually flavourful and fresh-tasting – even fruity – when young, becoming more pungent and firmer (but not hard) as they age. Fine examples are Gruyère, Pecorino and Gouda.
   Hard cheeses These cheeses have been pressed to remove as much whey from the curds as possible, which ensures a long shelf life. They are matured for several months, at least. Firm, hard varieties, such as Parmesan and vintage Cheddar may be matured for as long as 24 months. They are often made in huge wheels, which can weigh up to 90kg. Examples include Parmesan, Comté, Beaufort and Cheddar (though this may be classified as a semi-hard cheese if it is relatively young).

Brie de Meaux

Blue cheeses Ranging from mild to strong, these are veined cheeses, marbled with mould. The best-known blue cheeses made from cow's milk are Gorgonzola and Stilton. Roquefort, known as the French king of cheeses, is made from sheep's milk. The blue mould that develops inside the cheese is derived from the penicillin family. Moist blue cheeses are generally wrapped in foil so that the rind stays damp and sticky.

Flavoured cheeses These are hard or semi-hard cheeses that have fruit, spices and herbs added during the production process. The rind is often coloured, as in the Dutch Edam, Gouda and Nagelkaas. Popular flavoured cheeses in the UK are Cornish Yarg, Wensleydale with Cranberry and Double Gloucester with Chives. Smoked cheeses are assigned to this category.

Cheese quality classifications

In France there are over 1,000 different cheeses; in the UK there are now in excess of 700. Across the globe small artisan cheese-makers create an array of excellent cheeses, but, of course, most of the cheese on sale in supermarkets is mass-produced in factories. The way in which a cheese is produced determines its quality and price.

To help the consumer differentiate between cheeses, in terms of their production and quality, cheeses are designated to one of four classifications (*appellations*) in France:

• **Farmhouse cheeses** These are made from the milk on the farm premises within 24 hours of it being taken from the cow. The characteristics of the environment, or *terroir*, will produce a farmhouse cheese with a distinctive flavour. These are my favourite cheeses.

• **Artisanal cheeses** Producers of these cheeses use milk that comes from their own farm, possibly supplemented by milk from other nearby farms. These are often small enterprises. The cheeses are generally archetypal in flavour and are likely to be very good quality, without quite matching the pre-eminence of a farmhouse cheese.

• **Cooperative cheeses** These are produced in a dairy using milk that comes from several local farms. In some of these dairies the quantity of cheese produced is quite large.

• **Industrial cheeses** This is the largest and most common category. These cheeses are mostly mass-produced using pasteurised milk and are often destined for large-scale distribution. They have a standardised flavour and keep for longer than farmhouse or artisanal cheeses, but they do not hold any appeal for me.

Putting together a cheeseboard

First of all you need to take into account the season, particularly when it comes to your selection of fresh cheeses. The flavour and texture of a cheese is largely determined by the milk, the quality of which is affected by the food the animal is eating at the time. During the summer, cows, sheep and goats feed on pastures, which are generally lush at the start of the season, whereas their feed is largely hay during the winter months. Not surprisingly, fresh cheeses made in late spring and early summer tend to be more lively and interesting than those produced during the winter. This applies in particular to goat's and sheep's cheeses.

If possible, buy your cheese from a specialist cheese producer (in France a *maître fromager*) or cheese shop, or failing that from a supermarket or delicatessen that offers an extensive range of high-quality cheeses. A specialist cheese producer will have the advantage of an ageing cellar or cave (*cave d'affinage*) that can provide optimal conditions for the cheeses as they ripen. They will also be able to offer you the chance to sample a few cheeses that have caught your eye, and may even supply you with little labels to identify each different variety on your cheeseboard.

In a high-end restaurant, such as The Waterside, you will be offered a fine selection of cheeses and a knowledgeable waiter will be there to advise you. If you are entertaining at home, your choice will be determined largely by the number of guests. For four people, my advice would be to serve just one generous wedge of perfectly ripe cheese such as Brie de Meaux or Stilton, or a lovely piece of Comté. I always like to serve an odd, rather than even, number of cheeses. For six to eight guests, I'd probably offer five cheeses. For ten to twelve guests I would suggest serving seven cheeses at most, to avoid the choice becoming confusing.

Select a variety of cheeses from each the following categories:

• A fresh or white cheese, from the Loire valley, perhaps, where you can find a host of fresh goat's cheeses between three and seven days old. There is also a wonderful little English goat's cheese called Innes Button. This cheese will prepare your palate, much as in a wine tasting where you would start with a local wine before moving onto a *premier cru*, then a *grand cru*.
• A soft fresh cheese, with a natural rind such as a Saint-Pierre, Brocciu or Banon de Provence.
• A soft cheese with a bloomy rind, such as Sharpham Brie or Camembert.
• A soft cheese with a washed rind, such as Stinking Bishop, Vacherin Mont d'Or or Taleggio.

• A semi-firm hard cheese, such as Berkswell or Saint-Nectaire, or a hard cheese, such as Parmigiano Reggiano or Comté.

• A blue cheese, such as Gorgonzola, Stilton, Roquefort, Bleu des Causses or Fourme d'Ambert.

• A flavoured cheese, such as Cornish Yarg or Edam.

To appreciate their flavour to the full, cheeses should be served at room temperature. So, if they are stored in the fridge, you will need to take them out an hour or so before serving.

A cheese board should look appealing and have a sumptuous selection of cheeses, presented attractively. The actual board could be a large piece of slate, a beautiful piece of wood or a marble slab. If you have a few vine leaves or chestnut leaves to hand, you could use these to line the surface decoratively. Arrange some dried fruit (figs, apricots, dates, etc.), walnuts and hazelnuts around the cheeses.

On a separate dish, you could also offer a few little bunches of black or green grapes, some pears or apples, celery leaves, and a small dish of chutney. You can equally serve quince paste alongside, although it won't necessarily go with every cheese, or a little honey, which would be a perfect accompaniment to Parmesan.

Don't forget to provide several knives, to avoid using the same knife for all the cheeses. I also advise you to make a start on each cheese, as this will encourage your guests to dig in…

Offer an assortment of different breads: walnut, raisin or fig bread or even a lovely *pain de campagne* would go beautifully with your cheese. Provide a selection of biscuits too: water biscuits, very lightly sweetened oat biscuits and rye crackers, perhaps.

As for selecting a suitable wine or other drink to accompany cheese, there are no hard and fast rules. Red or white wine, *vin jaune*, whisky, sherry, port, Sauternes, cider and beer are all possibilities. It depends on the cheeses you have chosen to serve, and on your personal taste.

Savouring a cheeseboard with an appropriate drink is a wonderful, relaxing way to end a meal, but if you are serving a dessert you may prefer to offer the cheese first, as a palate-cleanser before the sweet finale. This is the tradition in France but the choice is yours.

If you want to amaze your friends, you could make cheese the focus of your meal. Try offering a tasting menu comprised entirely of cheeses, with a selection of seven to nine, from the mildest type to the strongest, each one accompanied by a different, appropriately selected drink. You might like to serve a few extra things alongside, such as cherry tomatoes, canapés, salami, etc… as well as a green salad dressed with a not-too-sharp lemon vinaigrette.

Bottom left:
Ardsallagh
smoked goat's
cheese

Bleu des Basques

Banon de Provence

Stilt

Tomme
de chèvre

Saint-Nectaire

Tomme
brûlée

Casanu

Reblochon

Valençay

Livarot

Morbier

Dôme de Vézelay

Pont
l'Évêque

Vieux-Lille

Fougerus

Tomme
d'Abondance

Mini-
baratte
affinée

Storing cheese

Cheese keeps best in its original paper or box, or wrapped in baking parchment or waxed paper. Avoid wrapping cheese in cling film, which forms a tight seal and prevents it from 'breathing', which has an adverse effect on the flavour. Vacuum-packed cheeses are convenient if you are travelling, but you should take them out of the vacuum pack as soon as you arrive at your destination, to let them breathe.

Some cheeses need cooler storage than others. Fresh cheeses need to be kept in the fridge. Soft and blue cheeses require cooler storage than hard cheeses, which are best kept in a cool larder (between 8 and 15°C). Ideally soft and blue cheeses should be stored between 5 and 8°C, or in the least cold part of the fridge (usually the salad drawer).

Don't forget to take cheese out of the fridge at least an hour before serving, and to trim the cut edges if they have already been started.

Cooking with cheese

Savouring cheese in its natural state – on its own, or with good bread or biscuits and perhaps a little fruit – is always a pleasure for me, but it is creating recipes with cheese that excites me the most. This is an ingredient that has so much to offer, in terms of flavour, texture and versatility. It is an essential component of many great classic dishes: fondue, gnudi, tartiflette and a host of omelettes, soufflés and pasta recipes. And it gives an incomparable savouriness to so many canapés, salads and snacks.

As I have developed and tested the recipes for this book, it has never failed to amaze me how the appropriate cheese can take a dish to new heights. It deepens and intensifies the taste of so many vegetable and meat dishes, adding to their nutritional value at the same time. After all, cheese is an excellent source of protein, B vitamins and minerals, especially calcium.

Some of the pairings are surprising too. Fish, for example, isn't an ingredient you would naturally put with cheese, but the combination can be sublime: try my grilled halibut steak with Parmesan and ginger hollandaise and you will believe me!

Even a little well-flavoured cheese can enhance a dish. At the most minimal level, I use it as a seasoning – like salt and pepper – to fine-tune many dishes. I hope my recipes will encourage you to explore the world of cheeses through cooking... there is so much to savour and enjoy. *Bon appetit*!

Gnudi (page 210)

Canapés

Comté

Lyonnaise soft cheese dip

Serves 6–8

200g fromage blanc, drained, or fromage frais

20g finely chopped shallot

10g finely snipped chives

1 tsp finely chopped garlic

15g finely chopped parsley

10g strong Dijon mustard

15ml red wine vinegar

25g olive oil

100g whipping cream, lightly whipped

Sea salt and freshly ground pepper

To serve

Thin slices of baguette, lightly toasted, or crostini

Grissini breadsticks

Cucumber batons

Raw baby carrots

Known as *cervelle de canut*, this dip originates from Lyon in France. My chef, Stéphane Colliet, who comes from the region, prepares it for guests at Le Miedzor, my restaurant in Crans-Montana in the Swiss Alps.

Put the fromage blanc into a bowl and mix in the shallot, chives, garlic and parsley. Add the mustard, wine vinegar and olive oil and mix again until the texture is uniform.

Finally, stir in the lightly whipped cream and season to taste with salt and pepper. Cover and chill until ready to serve.

To serve, spoon the dip into a small bowl and offer croûtes or crostini, grissini, cucumber batons and raw baby carrots, for dipping.

Celery with Roquefort butter and walnuts

SERVES 4

1 or 2 bunches of celery, depending on size

8 walnuts in their shell, fresh (wet) if in season, otherwise dried

250ml cold milk (only if using dried nuts)

100g butter, lightly softened

About 200g Roquefort or Stilton

This dish is lovely served as an *amuse-bouche* with a glass of Sauternes, or at the end of a meal with a glass of Port. Stilton pairs equally as well as Roquefort with the celery.

Using a small knife, cut off 2–3cm from the base of the celery bunch(es). One by one, remove the outer stalks (save these for stocks, soups etc.) keeping the most tender inner stalks, i.e. about half of the bunch. Soak these in iced water for about 10 minutes, then drain, wrap in a damp tea towel and refrigerate until needed.

Remove the walnuts from their shells (if using dried, keeping some in the shell for serving, if you like). If using fresh (wet) nuts, use the tip of the knife to remove the skins. Blanch dried walnuts, 2 or 3 at a time, in boiling water for 2 minutes, then use a knife tip to remove the skins, and immerse the nuts in the cold milk. Place in the fridge with the celery.

Put the softened butter into a bowl and crumble in enough of the cheese to give the strength of flavour required. Roughly mix together, using a fork.

Arrange the celery stems on a wooden cheese board, filling the hollows of these with the Roquefort butter. Keep a few stems unfilled and place the rest of the cheese on the board, so guests can help themselves accordingly. Drain the dried walnuts, if using, and add these or the fresh walnuts to the board, including any reserved dried nuts in shells.

Parmesan lace shells filled with goat's cheese

Makes 12

100g Parmigiano Reggiano, finely grated

80g fresh goat's cheese

20ml double cream

2 tsp finely snipped chives

12 small semi-confit cherry tomatoes (see page 248), optional

Sea salt and freshly ground pepper

This exquisite canapé is an explosion of sheer pleasure in the mouth. The Parmesan shells are very fragile and can break easily as you shape them from the oven, or fill them, so handle with great care.

Preheat the oven to 180°C/Gas 4.

Cut an empty egg box into 6 cups and wrap the outside of each cup with cling film. Place them hollow side down on your work surface.

Using half the grated Parmesan, carefully create 6 small mounds on a non-stick baking tray, spacing them well apart. Spread each out into a 5cm circle, 3mm thick. Bake in the oven for 3–4 minutes until lightly coloured and resembling cooked tuiles.

As soon as they are cooked, use a palette knife to lift each round and place it on an upturned, cling-film wrapped cup, so that they take on a slightly concave shape, like a little basket. Leave to cool.

As soon as the Parmesan shells are cold, very gently remove them from the egg box moulds. Keep in a dry place until ready to use or store in an airtight container for up to a day (thereafter they will start to lose their flavour). Repeat with the remaining Parmesan to make another 6 shells.

For the filling, mix the goat's cheese and cream together, season with salt and pepper to taste and stir in the chives.

Just before serving, divide the goat's cheese mixture between the 12 Parmesan shells and arrange a semi-confit tomato, if using, on top. Serve at once; allow two per person.

For a more uniform appearance, you can use a plain 6–8cm pastry cutter to cut out neat rounds as soon as the shells come out of the oven, if you prefer.

Gougères

MAKES 40–50

1 quantity choux pastry (see page 250)

100g Gruyère or Comté, grated

A pinch of cayenne pepper

A pinch of freshly grated nutmeg

A pinch of sweet paprika, plus extra to finish (optional)

Eggwash (1 medium egg mixed with 1 tsp milk)

These little cheese-flavoured choux buns are delicious served warm as a canapé or with pre-dinner drinks. You can also fill them with a spoonful of Mornay sauce (see page 246).

Preheat the oven to 180°C/Gas 4. Line a large baking sheet with baking parchment.

Make the choux pastry (following the method on page 250), and when the last egg has been absorbed and the mixture is smooth, add three-quarters of the grated cheese, the cayenne, nutmeg and paprika, if using, without working the mixture too much.

Put the pastry into a piping bag fitted with a 1cm plain nozzle, and pipe small mounds in staggered rows onto the lined baking sheet.

Brush with the eggwash and mark with a fork, then sprinkle the remaining grated cheese over the top. Bake in the oven for about 20 minutes until the choux buns are dry and crisp on the outside and base, but still soft inside. Transfer to a wire rack to cool slightly.

Arrange the gougères on a serving dish and serve warm, as they are or dusted with a light sprinkling of sweet paprika, if you like.

It isn't practical to make a smaller quantity of choux, but you can freeze the cooked gougères as soon as they have cooled if there are more than you need here; simply defrost at room temperature and reheat for 2 minutes in an oven preheated to 180°C/Gas 4.

Gougères, cheese straws (page 28) and mimolette sablés (page 29)

Cheese straws

MAKES 24

400g quick puff pastry (see page 249)

Plain flour, for dusting

Eggwash (1 egg yolk mixed with 1 tsp milk), to glaze

80g Emmenthal, Gruyère or Parmigiano Reggiano, freshly grated

1 tsp sweet paprika

A small pinch of cayenne pepper

These beautifully crisp *allumettes au fromage* are excellent with an aperitif, but can equally be served alongside a chicken consommé. (Illustrated on page 26.)

Line a baking sheet with baking parchment. Roll out the pastry on a lightly floured surface to a 28 x 12cm rectangle, about 2mm thick. Loosely roll the pastry over the rolling pin and unfurl it onto the prepared baking sheet. Refrigerate for 20 minutes.

Preheat the oven to 180°C/Gas 4.

Brush the entire surface of the pastry with eggwash and scatter the grated cheese evenly over the top. Mix the paprika and cayenne together and dust over the surface.

Using a large chef's knife, trim the pastry edges to neaten, then cut in half to give 2 pieces, each 14 x 12cm. Cut each piece into 1cm wide strips, to create 24 straws in total.

Either leave them plain or, using a palette knife, lift each straw off the baking sheet and twist the ends 6 times in opposite directions to create spirals.

Bake in the oven for 5–6 minutes until golden. As soon as they come out of the oven, carefully transfer the straws to a wire rack and leave to cool slightly.

Arrange the cheese straws in a tall tumbler or on a board, and serve, ideally still warm.

Mimolette sablés

250g plain flour

200g unsalted butter, cut into small dice

250g Mimolette, grated

Eggwash (1 medium egg mixed with 1 tsp milk)

12 blanched almonds, cut in half lengthways

These savoury sablé biscuits are easy to make and lovely served with an aperitif. You can of course use a pastry cutter to cut shaped sablés of your choice. If Mimolette is hard to find, use an aged Manchego instead. (Illustrated on page 26.)

Put the flour into a large bowl and rub in the butter until the mixture resembles coarse breadcrumbs. Add the grated cheese and mix well, without overworking, until the mixture is well combined and uniform.

Roll out the sablé dough on a large sheet of baking parchment, to a square, about 7mm thick, then cover with cling film and place in the fridge to rest for about 30 minutes.

Preheat the oven to 180°C/Gas 4.

Using a very sharp knife, cut the sablé dough into rectangles, about 2.5 x 5cm. Using a palette knife, lift the rectangles onto a baking sheet, leaving space in between them.

Brush the tops of the biscuits with eggwash, then place an almond half in the centre of each, pressing it in very lightly. Bake in the oven for 10 minutes or until the sablés take on a lightly golden colour. Transfer to a wire rack to cool.

Chicory leaves with Roquefort and rhubarb compote

SERVES 4-6

1 medium or 2 small rhubarb stems (about 100g in total)

40g caster sugar

3-4 tsp hot water

2 medium chicory bulbs (about 100g in total)

60g Roquefort, Stilton or Swedish Ädelost, crumbled or cut into small pieces

I adore the freshness of rhubarb with the pungency of a strong cheese, and this canapé is a lovely way to enjoy the contrast. Depending on the season, rhubarb can have more or less acidity, so to allow for this you might need to adjust the amount of sugar up or down.

Peel the rhubarb stem(s), rinse in cold water, dry well then cut into small cubes.

Sprinkle the sugar evenly into a dry heavy-based pan and warm over a gentle heat, stirring occasionally to ensure it melts and colours evenly. As soon as the sugar syrup turns a very light caramel colour, add the cubed rhubarb with 3-4 tsp hot water.

Cook over a gentle heat, stirring from time to time, until the rhubarb is softened but still holding its shape; this will take 3-5 minutes, depending on how tender the fruit is. Transfer to a large bowl, cover with cling film and set aside to cool.

Remove the outermost leaves from the chicory bulbs, shred these and set aside. Separate out and trim the inner leaves, shaping the end of each leaf into a point. If necessary, gently wash the leaves.

To serve, arrange the chicory leaves in a circle on a large dish, spoon a little rhubarb into each leaf and top with a couple of pieces of blue cheese. Pile the shredded chicory into the middle, scatter over the remaining cheese and serve.

Brie-filled mini seaweed scones

Makes about 18

135g 'type 55' plain white flour, plus extra for dusting

25g butter, softened

20g caster sugar

12g baking powder

¼ tsp fine sea salt, plus a pinch for the glaze

15g dried seaweed (sea lettuce or dulse), rinsed in cold water, patted dry and finely chopped

35ml milk

40g double cream

Eggwash (1 egg yolk mixed with 1 tsp milk), to glaze

200g well-ripened Brie, rind removed

To serve

180g dried seaweed (a mixture of sea lettuce and Japanese red algae), rinsed in cold water, patted dry and cut into pieces

2 tbsp light olive oil

Juice of 1 lemon

Freshly ground pepper

These little scones have a mild briny flavour, reminiscent of the sea, and make a novel *amuse-bouche*. Many countries and regions outside France – from Australia to England – now make excellent Brie. You could, however, use another soft-rind cheese that is flavoursome without being too strong.

To make the scones, put the flour, butter, sugar, baking powder and salt into the bowl of a stand mixer and mix on a low speed to a rough dough. Add the chopped seaweed and mix for 30 seconds, then add the milk and cream and mix again, still on a low speed, for about 3–4 minutes to a homogeneous dough.

Bring the dough back into the middle of the bowl and then mix for another minute. Shape into a ball, wrap in cling film and refrigerate for at least 30 minutes.

Line a baking sheet with baking parchment. Roll out the chilled dough on a lightly floured surface to a 1cm thickness and cut out rounds, using a 3cm plain pastry cutter. Turn the rounds over onto the lined baking sheet, arranging them in staggered rows.

Add a pinch of salt to the egg glaze and brush over the top of the scones. Leave to stand at warm room temperature (20–24°C) for 20 minutes. Meanwhile, preheat the oven to 180°C/Gas 4.

Bake the scones in the oven for 7–8 minutes until risen and lightly golden on top. Transfer to a wire rack and leave to cool.

Using a serrated knife, cut each scone horizontally through the middle, about three-quarters of the way across. Place about 10g Brie inside each scone and close the tops.

To serve, toss the seaweed with the olive oil, lemon juice and some pepper (don't add salt as seaweed is already salty). Allow 3 scones per person and serve the seaweed in a bowl on the side.

Gruyère croûtes

MAKES 16

60g unsalted butter

4 slices of white sandwich loaf (about 10cm square), crusts removed

1 medium egg

80g Gruyère, grated (on a medium grater)

40ml double cream

2 tsp kirsch

A knifetip of freshly grated nutmeg

Freshly ground pepper

16 flat-leaf parsley sprigs, to garnish

The simplest ideas are often the best, as these delightful *croûtes genovoises* demonstrate. The more aged the cheese the more flavoursome they will be. This recipe can also be served as a starter, in which case keep the toast slices whole, and increase the time in the oven to 6 minutes.

Heat the butter in a large frying pan over a medium heat. Add the slices of bread and brown them lightly on the underside for 1 minute, then turn over and cook the other side, without letting them take on too much colour. Drain on kitchen paper then cut each slice into 4 squares. Place on a small baking tray.

Preheat the oven to 200°C/Gas 6.

Lightly beat the egg in a bowl, then add the grated Gruyère and mix with a fork. Add the cream then finally mix in the kirsch, nutmeg and a little pepper.

Using either a teaspoon or a piping bag fitted with a medium nozzle, divide the mixture between the 16 fried bread squares, placing it in little mounds. Bake in the oven for 3–4 minutes until slightly puffed and turning lightly golden.

Using a palette knife, transfer the croûtes to a warmed platter. Top each with a parsley sprig and serve. Allow 4 croûtes per person.

Pork and cheese empanadas

Makes 14–16

For the pastry

360g flan pastry or puff pastry
trimmings (see page 249)

Plain flour, for dusting

1 egg white, lightly beaten,
for sealing

For the filling

150ml groundnut oil

250g pork shoulder or neck,
trimmed of fat and minced using
a medium setting

1 onion (about 150g), finely
chopped

2 garlic cloves, finely chopped

150g tomatoes, peeled, deseeded
and finely diced

A generous pinch each of ground
cumin, dried oregano and sweet
paprika

A small pinch of chilli powder

1 tsp fine sea salt

1 tsp freshly ground pepper

300ml veal stock (shop-bought),
or home-made rich chicken stock
(see page 244)

150g Cheddar, Cantal or Edam
cheese, freshly grated

75g cottage cheese

There are numerous empanada recipes, and my favourites are made with pork or beef. You can use chicken for this recipe if you prefer, substituting a cheese with a milder flavour, such as mild Cheddar or Tilsit. The empanadas can be frozen raw in an airtight container, for up to 2–3 weeks; allow to thaw completely before baking.

To make the filling, heat 100ml of the oil in a frying pan. Add the minced pork and brown it evenly over a high heat, then transfer to a colander to drain off the fat.

Heat the remaining oil in a sauté pan over a medium heat, add the onion and sweat for 2–3 minutes, then add the garlic and tomatoes and cook for 15 minutes, stirring every 5 minutes. Add the browned pork, cumin, oregano, paprika, chilli powder, salt, pepper and stock. Cook over a low heat for 40 minutes, then add the grated cheese and cottage cheese and cook for another minute or two, stirring with a wooden spoon.

Transfer the mixture to a bowl, cover with cling film and pierce it in several places with the tip of a sharp knife. Set aside to cool, then refrigerate until ready to use.

Roll out the pastry on a lightly floured surface to a 1.5mm thickness and cut out rounds, using a 9cm plain cutter. Gather the trimmings and roll out to cut more rounds. Place a generous tablespoonful (about 20g) of the chilled filling in the centre of a pastry round and brush the pastry edges with a little egg white.

Fold the pastry over the filling to make a turnover and pinch the edges together between your thumb and forefinger, giving the border a quarter-turn inwards every 5mm to create a plaited effect edge and seal it completely. Repeat with the remaining filling and pastry circles. Place the empanadas on a baking tray and refrigerate for 20 minutes.

Preheat the oven to 180°C/Gas 4. Bake the empanadas in the oven for 13–15 minutes until golden. Transfer to a wire rack to cool a little.

Serve the empanadas hot or warm, arranging them in a basket. Or, for a fun presentation, offer them around in little paper cones.

Farandole of sweet and savoury spoonfuls

SERVES 4

This canapé is a visual delight as well as a gastronomic one, with each spoon offering a distinctive flavour sensation. You could create your own spoons, including your favourite cheese, fruit or vegetables, and varying them according to the season. I like to serve two of each spoon to every guest. Assemble them just before serving.

For the semi-confit cherry tomatoes and Greek yoghurt

A little olive oil

24 small cherry tomatoes

140g Greek yoghurt

Thyme and/or snipped tarragon leaves, to finish

Sea salt and freshly ground pepper

For the green olive tapenade and goat's cheese

140g green olive tapenade (see page 248 for home-made)

60g fresh goat's cheese, cut into small dice or crumbled

Extra virgin olive oil, to drizzle

Oregano sprigs, to finish

For the fig, prosciutto and mascarpone

2 very ripe figs, ideally red

40g prosciutto

120g mascarpone

For the melon, cherry jam and Mimolette

140g Cavaillon (Cantaloupe) melon

140g good-quality cherry preserve (ideally with whole cherries)

40g Mimolette (aged for 12–18 months), pared into shavings

For the cherry tomato and yoghurt spoons, heat the oil in a small pan, add the cherry tomatoes and cook gently for 5 minutes to semi-confit. Transfer to a plate and leave to cool. Divide the yoghurt between 8 spoons and top each with 3 semi-confit tomatoes. Sprinkle with the herb(s) and grind over some salt and pepper.

For the olive tapenade spoons, divide the tapenade between 8 spoons, top with the goat's cheese and drizzle over a little extra virgin olive oil. Garnish with oregano sprigs and sprinkle with a little pepper.

For the fig, prosciutto and mascarpone spoons, cut the figs into small dice and the prosciutto into very fine slivers. Divide the mascarpone between 8 spoons and top with the figs and prosciutto.

For the melon and cherry spoons, scoop the melon into small spheres, using a melon baller, or cut into small cubes. Combine with the cherry preserve and cheese shavings and divide between 8 spoons.

Simply arrange the spoons on individual plates or a large platter to serve.

Soups

Stilton

Gazpacho with goat's cheese stuffed cherry tomatoes

SERVES 6

400g plump, nicely ripe tomatoes, roughly chopped

2 red peppers, cored, deseeded and finely sliced

1 small onion (75g), finely sliced

1 cucumber, peeled, halved, deseeded and finely sliced

1 garlic clove, finely sliced

½ slice of white sandwich loaf, cut into small dice

1 small basil sprig, plus 6 extra sprigs to garnish

3 drops of Tabasco

75ml virgin olive oil

Sea salt and freshly ground pepper

For the stuffed tomatoes

18 medium cherry tomatoes

1 Chabichou goat's cheese, cut into small pieces

1 small onion (75g), finely chopped

1½ tbsp fresh white (day-old) breadcrumbs

10g mixed basil, flat-leaf parsley and chives, finely chopped together

1 egg yolk

2 tbsp virgin olive oil

I like to use Chabichou du Poitou here. Made from fresh goat's cheese, this mould-ripened creamy cheese has a delicious sharp flavour, which becomes more pronounced as it matures. You can substitute any soft-ripened goat's cheese with a comparable flavour, such as a crottin or Valençay. I have often served this gazpacho in this way as a lunch dish at The Waterside Inn, to the delight of our guests.

To make the gazpacho, put all the ingredients, except the olive oil and seasoning, into a bowl and stir to mix. Cover with cling film and refrigerate for 6–12 hours.

For the stuffed tomatoes, preheat the oven to 180°C/Gas 4. Slice off the top third of each cherry tomato; save these 'lids'. Using a teaspoon, scoop out the insides of each tomato (the seeds and a little of the flesh) and set aside.

Put the goat's cheese into a bowl with the onion, breadcrumbs, herbs, egg yolk and half the olive oil, and mix with a fork. Season with pepper to taste.

Generously fill the cherry tomatoes with the mixture, then replace the lids. Place in a shallow ovenproof dish or on a baking tray and brush with the remaining olive oil. Bake for 12–15 minutes until the tomatoes are two-thirds cooked and the stuffing is very hot.

Transfer the chilled gazpacho ingredients to a food processor or blender and blitz for no more than 2 minutes, to avoid the mixture turning pale – you want the gazpacho to be a good red colour.

Add the olive oil, then strain the mixture through a fine chinois or sieve, pressing down with the back of a ladle to extract the liquid. Season with salt and pepper to taste.

To serve, divide the chilled gazpacho between 6 chilled shallow bowls, then arrange 3 hot stuffed cherry tomatoes in each. Garnish with basil sprigs and serve at once.

Normandy onion soup

SERVES 4

70g butter

400g onions, rinsed in cold water and finely sliced

250ml medium cider

1 small bouquet garni (thyme sprig, bay leaf and a few parsley stalks, tied together)

30g plain flour

650ml chicken stock (see page 244)

12–16 slices of baguette, cut at an angle, about 3mm thick

70ml double cream

30g Gruyère, mature Cheddar or Comté, grated

Sea salt and freshly ground pepper

You can turn this *soupe à l'oignon, gratinée à la normande* into an onion soup *à la lyonnaise* if you replace the cider with white wine. The flavours will just be a little different. My personal preference is for the sweet element that the cider brings, but the choice is yours. To make it suitable for vegetarians, simply replace the chicken stock with water.

Melt 40g of the butter in a fairly deep frying pan or sauté pan over a medium heat. Add the onions and sweat for 2 minutes, then increase the heat slightly and cook until lightly golden. Add 150ml of the cider and the bouquet garni and simmer for 5 minutes. Remove from the heat and set aside.

Melt the remaining 30g butter in a saucepan, add the flour and cook over a gentle heat for 2 minutes, stirring constantly with a whisk, to make a blond roux. Add the stock and bring to the boil, still stirring with the whisk. Cook over a gentle heat for 15 minutes.

Add the onion and cider mixture to the thickened stock and simmer for another 15 minutes, skimming the surface every few minutes. Remove the bouquet garni and season the soup with salt and pepper to taste; keep hot.

Meanwhile, for the croûtes, preheat the grill to high or the oven to 180°C/Gas 4. Toast the slices of baguette under the hot grill or in the oven for a few minutes until golden on both sides. (If using the oven rather than the grill to gratinée the soup, increase the setting to 200°C/Gas 6.)

To serve, pour the remaining cider equally into 4 warmed ovenproof bowls, then divide the onion soup between them. Spoon the cream on top and lay the croûtes on the surface. Sprinkle with the Gruyère and place under the grill (or in the oven) for a few minutes until gratinéed. Serve at once, while piping hot.

Cream of broccoli and Stilton soup

SERVES 6

350g tender, green broccoli

50g butter

1 onion (100g), sliced into rings

100g potatoes, peeled and diced

1.5 litres water

100g Stilton or Fourme d'Ambert cheese, cut into small pieces

Juice of 1 lemon

Sea salt and freshly ground pepper

To finish

100g flaked almonds

150g whipping cream

This gently hued soup has a nicely balanced flavour, and the crunch of the almonds adds a delightful contrast.

Peel the broccoli stems and pick off a dozen very small florets, about 100g in total. Blanch these in boiling water for 30 seconds, then refresh and set aside. Roughly chop the rest of the broccoli.

Heat the butter in a flameproof casserole or pan over a medium heat. Add the onion and sweat for 2 minutes, then add the chopped broccoli and potatoes. Cook for 2–3 minutes, then pour in the water, season lightly with salt and cook at a low simmer for 30 minutes. Add the cheese and cook for 2–3 minutes.

Working in batches, process the soup in a blender for 2–3 minutes, then strain through a chinois into a clean pan; keep hot.

Just before serving, add the lemon juice to the soup and season with salt and pepper to taste. Lightly toast the flaked almonds and whip the cream until thick enough to hold a ribbon.

Divide the reserved blanched broccoli florets between warmed bowls or soup plates and pour on the hot soup. Spoon the lightly whipped cream on top of the soup and scatter over the toasted flaked almonds. Serve at once.

Tarhana soup

Serves 4

250g tarhana crackers, or tarhana granules (see note)

600ml vegetable stock (see page 245) or water

Juice of ½ lemon

Sea salt and freshly ground pepper

To finish

150g feta

4 tsp light olive oil

Of Greek-Cypriot origin, this nourishing soup also appears on menus in Turkey and Greece. It can be served at any meal, from breakfast to lunch, even dinner. Its thickness varies from region to region, with more or less liquid added. The feta can be replaced with halloumi: cut into cubes and fry in foaming butter until golden, then scatter over the soup.

If using tarhana crackers, soak them in cold water to cover for an hour, then drain.

Pour the stock or water into a pan, add the drained crackers or tarhana granules and bring to the boil over a medium heat. As soon as it comes to the boil, lower the heat and cook gently at a bare simmer, stirring every 5 minutes or so, for an hour if using crackers or 25 minutes for granules. Season to taste with salt and pepper and add the lemon juice.

To serve, divide the soup between 4 warmed shallow bowls. Crumble over the feta and finish with delicate drops of olive oil.

You can buy ready-made tarhana crackers and tarhana granules in grocers specialising in Cypriot, Greek or Turkish products.

Courgette soup with Cancoillotte

SERVES 4

25ml light olive oil

½ tsp cumin seeds, or a generous pinch of curry powder

1 onion (100g), very finely chopped

1 small garlic clove, finely chopped

500g courgettes, trimmed and cut into fine rounds

500ml boiling water, salted

75g Cancoillotte cheese

Sea salt and freshly ground pepper

For the courgette flowers
(optional)

4 courgette flowers

Virgin sesame or groundnut oil, for deep-frying

25g cornflour

90g plain flour

½ tsp bicarbonate of soda

A good pinch of fleur de sel (flaky sea salt)

About 120ml good-quality sparkling water, chilled

Cancoillotte, originating in the Haute-Saône area of the Franche-Comté region, has a thick, runny consistency and is served with a spoon. If you are unable to find it, you can use Vache-qui-rit (laughing cow cheese) instead. When in season, courgette flowers – tempura-coated and deep-fried – will enhance this soup considerably.

Heat the olive oil in a pan over a medium heat, add the cumin seeds or curry powder and cook for 1–2 minutes if using cumin seeds, 1 minute for curry powder. Add the onion and garlic, lower the heat and cook, stirring, until the onion is translucent, about 3–4 minutes.

Add the courgettes and stir to mix with the onion. Increase the heat and cook for 3–4 minutes, without letting the courgettes take on any colour. Slowly pour in the salted boiling water and cook over a medium heat for 20 minutes.

Meanwhile, if serving tempura courgette flowers, gently open up the flowers and, using a small knife, remove the stamen and the sepals (these are found at the base of each flower where it joins to the courgette). Cut off the end of each flower at the base.

Heat the oil for deep-frying in a suitable deep, heavy pan to 170°C. For the tempura batter, mix the cornflour, flour, bicarbonate of soda and sea salt together in a bowl. Add the sparkling water a little at a time, stirring with chopsticks but mixing only lightly; there will be little lumps in the mixture, but this is as it should be. The batter should be just thick enough to lightly coat the chopsticks; it needs to be used immediately.

When the oil is ready, one at a time, pick up the courgette flowers with chopsticks and dip them into the batter to barely cover then drop into the hot oil. Cook for about 1 minute until golden, turning once so that they colour evenly; they are ready as soon as they float to the surface. Remove and drain on kitchen paper.

When the soup is ready, remove from the heat and stir in the cheese. Transfer to a blender or food processor and blitz for about 3 minutes until velvety smooth. Strain the soup through a fine chinois or sieve, add salt and pepper to taste and serve at once, in soup bowls with the tempura courgette flowers, if serving, on the side.

Puy lentil velouté with Grana Padano

SERVES 6–8

100g butter

1 medium-large onion (150g), sliced into rings

150g carrots, sliced into rounds

2 garlic cloves, chopped

1 clove, crushed

150g piece of salted pork belly, blanched and cut into 2 or 3 pieces

A bouquet garni (½ leek, 2 thyme sprigs and 2 bay leaves, tied together)

2 litres water

300g Puy green lentils

150g Grana Padano (aged for 2–3 years) or Parmigiano Reggiano, grated

150ml double cream

Sea salt and freshly ground pepper

I generally use one of the hard cheeses listed here for this satisfying soup, but you can use Gouda or a slightly aged Tomme de Béarn, diced. You could also serve a Comté espuma on the side in small glasses (see page 54), in which case reduce the quantity of cheese in the velouté to 50g.

Melt the butter in a large saucepan, add the onion and sweat over a medium heat for 2–3 minutes, stirring with a wooden spoon. Add the carrots, garlic, crushed clove and pieces of pork. Cook over a medium heat for 5 minutes, stirring every minute. Add the bouquet garni, then pour in the water and bring to the boil.

Meanwhile, put the lentils into a separate pan and pour on enough cold water to cover generously. Bring to the boil, skim if necessary and cook for 2–3 minutes, then drain.

When the soup comes to the boil, add the drained lentils and cook over a gentle heat for about 40 minutes until the lentils are tender. Stir in the cheese and cream and simmer for a further 5 minutes.

Take the pan off the heat and remove and discard the bouquet garni. Using a skimmer, lift out the pieces of pork and set aside.

Working in batches, process the soup in a blender for 2–3 minutes until smooth, then strain through a chinois into a clean pan. Season with salt and pepper to taste; keep hot.

Cut the belly pork into small pieces, discarding the rind, and divide between warmed bowls or soup plates. Pour in the hot velouté and serve at once.

Chestnut soup with Comté espuma

SERVES 6

20ml light olive oil

1 onion (100g), cut into large dice

50g celeriac (ideally) or celery, cut into large dice

500g vacuum-packed, cooked, peeled chestnuts, rinsed and drained

125ml dry Champagne or sparkling wine

1 litre chicken or vegetable stock (see pages 244–5)

100ml milk

Sea salt and freshly ground pepper

For the Comté espuma

500ml whole milk

500ml double cream

100g Comté cheese (aged for 18–24 months), grated

A small pinch of cayenne pepper

For the garnish

2 firm, medium ceps

2 tbsp light olive oil

3 plump scallops, sliced in half horizontally (optional)

This exquisite soup is perfect for a special occasion, with the espuma adding a decadent finish. Make the soup a day ahead, leaving the espuma (which calls for a whipping siphon) and ceps to prepare before serving. (Illustrated on previous page.)

Heat the olive oil in a pan. Add the onion and celeriac or celery, and sweat over a low heat for 3–4 minutes, stirring occasionally. Add the chestnuts and two-thirds of the Champagne or wine and cook over a medium heat for 5 minutes. Add the stock and cook until the chestnuts collapse easily when pressed with a fork. Add the milk and some seasoning, and cook for another 2 minutes. Take off the heat.

Working in fairly small batches, blitz the soup in a blender for about 2 minutes until smooth, then strain through a fine chinois into a clean pan and set aside, covered to keep hot.

For the espuma, pour the milk and cream into a pan and slowly bring to the boil. Remove from the heat, add the grated Comté then blend to a creamy consistency. Season with salt, pepper and cayenne. Pour into the chamber of a whipping siphon, making sure it doesn't come above the maximum level mark. Screw the top on to close the siphon, put the gas canister in the cartridge holder, then screw the base of it onto the siphon. This will puncture the canister and you will hear gas go into the chamber. Unscrew and remove the cartridge holder. Stand the siphon upright in a bain-marie at 50°C until needed.

For the garnish, using a small knife, pare the cep stalks and wipe the caps clean with damp kitchen paper, to remove all traces of grit and sand. Cut each cep into 6 slices. Heat the olive oil in a large frying pan, add the ceps and fry for 2 minutes on each side, until golden. Set aside on kitchen paper, sprinkling with salt and pepper to taste.

Cook the halved scallops, if using, in the same frying pan, without moving for 45 seconds, then turn them over and cook the other side for 30 seconds. Remove and set aside with the ceps.

Divide the remaining Champagne or wine between 6 shallow bowls, then pour in the hot chestnut soup. Top each serving with 2 cep slices and a scallop disc, if using. Take the siphon, turn it upside down and shake vigorously. Press the button and finish each soup with a generous rosette of Comté espuma. Serve at once.

Leek and potato velouté with soft Tomme cheese

SERVES 6

250g leeks, trimmed, outer layer and darker green parts removed, well washed

60g butter

1 small onion (80g), sliced into rings

200g potatoes, cut into cubes

1 thyme sprig

1.5 litres chicken or vegetable stock (see pages 244–5)

50g double cream

100g Tomme de l'Aubrac cheese, or another soft cheese, cut into slivers

A bunch of chives, snipped

Sea salt and freshly ground pepper

This velouté is a vichyssoise, with slivers of soft, fresh Tomme de l'Aubrac, added just before serving. The cheese melts into the soup, with palate-pleasing results. If you cannot find this cheese you can use another soft tomme, or Raclette, or a young Gruyère (aged for 6–12 months).

Chop the leeks into small pieces. Melt the butter in a pan over a medium heat. Add the onion and leeks and sweat for 5 minutes, stirring occasionally. Add the potatoes and thyme, then pour in the stock. Season lightly with salt and simmer gently for 30 minutes. Remove the thyme sprig.

Add the cream and remove from the heat. Working in small batches, blitz the soup in a blender for 2–3 minutes and transfer to a clean pan; keep hot. Season with salt and pepper to taste.

To serve, pour the velouté into warmed bowls or soup plates and scatter over the slivers of cheese, dividing them equally. Sprinkle generously with snipped chives and serve at once.

Starters & Snacks

Montgomery Cheddar

Artichokes with fromage blanc and salmon roe

4 Breton globe artichokes
(400–500g each)

Juice of 1 lemon, plus ½ lemon,
cut in half

120g fromage blanc

A splash of cold milk (if needed)

75g rocket or watercress leaves

100g salmon trout or salmon roe

Sea salt and freshly ground
pepper

4 slices of pain de campagne
bread, toasted, to serve

In the middle of their season, artichokes are fleshy with a pronounced hazelnut flavour, marrying beautifully with the fromage blanc and fish roe in this exquisite starter. You can use Greek yoghurt instead of fromage blanc if you prefer, or if you can't find the latter.

Fill a pan large enough to take the artichokes with water and bring to the boil. Meanwhile, break off the stems from the artichokes and remove the fibrous part from the base of the hearts. Using a serrated knife, cut off the tops of the leaves. Remove the outer layer of leaves at the base of the hearts, by twisting and pulling them off one at a time.

Wash the prepared artichoke hearts in plenty of water, then add them to the boiling water with a large pinch of salt and the halved lemon half. Cook at a low boil for 30–45 minutes, depending on size, adding a little more boiling water if necessary during cooking to keep the artichokes submerged. To check that each one is cooked, gently pull an artichoke leaf; it should come away easily. Drain and refresh in cold water, then drain and set aside.

Add the lemon juice to the fromage blanc, with just a little salt, and pepper to taste, and stir to combine evenly. If the mixture seems a little thick, add the splash of milk.

Slide a spoon down inside the leaves in the middle of each artichoke and push it down as far as the heart, then turn it right around the artichoke to release the heart from the leaves. Use the spoon to remove the choke from each heart. Remove the top leaves from each artichoke and set aside, then replace the heart in the artichoke.

To serve, divide the rocket or watercress between 4 large plates and place the artichokes in the middle, with the reserved top leaves arranged around each in a circle. Spoon the fromage blanc mixture into the artichoke hearts and top with the fish roe. Give each guest a small plate so they can discard the non-edible part of the leaves. Serve cold (but not chilled), with warm toast.

Sautéed prawns with feta and basil

SERVES 4

8 raw king prawns in shell, about 60g each

150ml light olive oil

1 small red pepper, cored, deseeded and cut into julienne

4 small basil sprigs

150g feta, cut into 1.5cm cubes

A pinch of ground Espelette pepper

Sea salt

1 lemon, cut into wedges, to serve

Simple and full of flavour, this rustic starter is a feast for the eyes and taste buds alike. You'll need to use fingers to shell the prawns, so provide finger bowls and plenty of napkins.

Rinse the prawns under cold running water, drain, then gently pat dry using kitchen paper.

Heat the olive oil in a large frying pan over a medium-high heat. When it is very hot, add the prawns and sprinkle them lightly with salt. Cook for 1 minute, then quickly turn them over with tongs or a fork and add the red pepper. Cook for 30 seconds, then add the basil sprigs and cook for another 30 seconds.

Scatter over the feta cubes and dust with the Espelette pepper. Cook, turning the prawns with a palette knife, for a final minute. Transfer to a large dish and serve at once, with lemon wedges.

Feta is the best known and most popular of all Greek cheeses. Made from sheep's or goat's milk, this creamy soft white cheese is traditionally kept in brine, which gives it a unique salty taste and crumbly texture. In 2002 feta was given protected origin status and it can now only be produced in Greece, though similar cheeses are produced in other countries.

Börek

Makes 6

15g dill leaves

15g flat-leaf parsley leaves

20g mint leaves

160g feta, crumbled

A generous pinch of freshly grated nutmeg

100ml light olive oil

6 sheets of ready-made filo pastry, 30 x 18cm

Freshly ground pepper

To serve (optional)

Vegetable oil for deep-frying

20g curly-leaf parsley

Sea salt

A truly Mediterranean snack, best served warm. I often choose to sprinkle a few drops of lemon juice over these delectable pastries as I eat them.

Preheat the oven to 180°C/Gas 4.

Finely snip the dill, parsley and mint leaves and put them into a bowl with the feta. Mix gently with a fork then add the nutmeg, a generous grind of pepper and a drizzle of olive oil and mix until evenly combined.

Cut the sheets of filo lengthways in half, to give you 12 strips, each 30 x 9cm. Brush one strip with olive oil, then lay another strip on top and brush this with a little oil. Spread a little of the feta and herb mixture over the surface.

Now fold the pastry over a little from the 4 corners so that the filling won't escape as you roll. Roll the strip up lengthways without applying any pressure. Place the feta roll on a baking tray, with the join underneath. Repeat the process with the remaining filo strips and filling, to shape 6 börek in total, spacing them apart on the baking tray.

Brush the börek all over with olive oil, including the ends, which will be open, to help prevent the filling escaping during cooking. Bake in the oven for 15–20 minutes until crisp and golden. Using a palette knife, transfer the börek to a wire rack to cool slightly.

Meanwhile, if preparing the fried parsley garnish, heat the oil in a deep, heavy pan to 180°C then add the parsley sprigs and fry for about 30 seconds until crisp. Remove with a slotted spoon, drain on kitchen paper and sprinkle with a little salt.

To serve, arrange the warm börek in a little stack or lattice pattern, and sprinkle with the fried parsley, if using.

Parmesan and Fontina flan

SERVES 6

2 medium eggs

100ml single cream

200ml double cream

100g Fontina, freshly grated

30g Parmigiano Reggiano, freshly grated

A pinch of freshly grated nutmeg

20g butter, softened

Sea salt and freshly ground pepper

This light and delicate flan slips down with alarming ease. I like to serve it barely set in the centre, with gently seasoned rocket, watercress or other peppery salad leaves on the side. Accompanied by toasted rustic bread and a tomato salad, it also makes a delicious light lunch.

Preheat the oven to 160°C/Gas 3.

Beat the eggs in a large bowl with a fork, as you would for an omelette. Add both creams and beat again until nicely combined. Stir in both grated cheeses, then season to taste with the nutmeg, pepper and just a very little salt.

Brush the base and sides of a ceramic baking dish, about 20cm in diameter and 3–4cm deep, with the butter. Add a sprinkling of salt and pepper, then pour the creamy mixture into the dish.

Stand this dish in a larger, shallow ovenproof dish lined with greaseproof paper. Pour enough just-boiled water into the larger dish to come halfway up the sides of the flan dish.

Bake in the oven for 10 minutes then lower the oven setting to 140°C/Gas 1 and cook for another 20 minutes. Check to see if the flan is cooked: it should be just set around the edges and lightly quivering in the middle. Lift the flan dish out of the water and place on a wire rack to cool.

The flan can be served warm or at room temperature, but not chilled or hot. Simply present it in its dish at the table and everyone can help themselves.

Goyères

SERVES 4

For the dough

200g plain flour, plus extra
for dusting

2 pinches of soft brown sugar

A good pinch of sea salt

10g fresh yeast

2½ tbsp warm milk

2 medium eggs, beaten

70g butter, melted and cooled
to warm

For the filling

100g ripe Gorgonzola or Fourme
d'Ambert, thickest part of crust
removed

2 medium eggs, beaten

100ml crème fraîche

16 walnut halves

Sea salt and freshly ground
pepper

To serve (optional)

A few escarole or chicory leaves

These individual savoury tarts are a speciality of northern France. Maroilles is the traditional cheese used but I prefer a more full-flavoured refined blue, such as Gorgonzola or Fourme d'Ambert. These go better with the walnuts that I like to include.

Put the flour into a large bowl with the sugar and salt. In a small bowl, cream the yeast with the milk until smooth, then add to the flour with the eggs. Mix together using your fingertips, pouring in the melted butter as you do so, until you have a soft, smooth, homogeneous dough.

Divide the dough into 4 equal portions then shape each into a ball, dusting with a little flour to stop the dough sticking to your fingers.

Place the dough balls on a baking tray, spacing them well apart. Starting from the centre and working outwards, spread each ball out to a round, about 10cm in diameter and 5mm thick, dipping your fingers in flour every now and then.

Set aside in a warm place (22–24°C) for 1 hour, by which time the dough should have almost doubled in volume. Meanwhile, preheat the oven to 200°C/Gas 6.

For the filling, put the cheese into a bowl and crush it with a fork, then add the beaten eggs, crème fraîche and plenty of pepper. Mix well to combine.

Lightly press down the centres of the goyère bases, leaving a 1.5cm raised border. Divide the filling between the bases and spread it out with a spoon, starting from the centre and stopping at the raised border. Arrange 4 walnut halves on each.

Bake the little tarts in the oven for 14–15 minutes until golden. Immediately slide them onto a wire rack, using a palette knife, and allow to cool slightly. Serve while still warm, accompanied, if you like, with crisp salad leaves.

Mexican tacos with Cheddar

Serves 6

100ml grapeseed oil

250g beef or venison fillet, cut into small dice

1 garlic clove, finely chopped

A pinch of ground cumin

1 quantity barbecue sauce (see page 247, or shop-bought)

12 shop-bought corn taco shells, 14cm long with a 6cm opening

400g tomatoes, peeled, deseeded and diced

200g onions (ideally red), cut into small dice

1 avocado, sliced or diced just before assembling

100g soured cream

200g baby gem or iceberg lettuce leaves, finely shredded

100–140g Cheddar or Monterey Jack, to taste, coarsely grated

Sea salt

In Mexico, tacos are popular street food – typically served filled with minced meat that is cooked until quite dry. When I tasted them, I resolved to come up with a better result, using succulent meat to make them more appetising. Fillet of beef or venison works a treat and you only need a small quantity. If you are lucky enough to be able to source Mexican queso añejo or queso blanco, use it – cut into fine slices – in place of the Cheddar.

Heat the oil in a frying pan over a high heat. Add the diced beef or venison and sauté for 2–3 minutes, depending on your preference for rare or well-cooked meat. Add the garlic and cumin, season lightly with salt and transfer to a bowl; set aside in a warm place.

Heat the barbecue sauce in a pan and let bubble to reduce if necessary to thicken to the consistency of a coulis; keep warm.

Preheat the oven to 80°C/Gas lowest setting. Put the taco shells on a baking tray and warm through in the oven for 3–4 minutes – no longer or they will be brittle rather than warm.

Meanwhile, in a bowl, mix the tomatoes with the onions, avocado and a little of the soured cream.

To serve, put a little shredded lettuce into each taco shell, then spoon in some of the tomato mixture. Add the meat to the barbecue sauce and warm through gently for a minute, then divide between the taco shells. Scatter the cheese generously over the top.

Serve at once, allowing 2 tacos per person, with the remaining barbecue sauce and soured cream on the side for guests to help themselves if they would like more.

Crique

500g medium potatoes

1 medium egg, lightly beaten

1 garlic clove, finely chopped

20g flat-leaf parsley, finely snipped

50ml grapeseed or groundnut oil

100g clarified butter

3 Picodon goat's cheeses (from Ardèche), soft in the middle, cut in half horizontally

Sea salt and freshly ground pepper

I adore this dish from the Ardèche, known as *crique ardéchoise*. The crispness of the potatoes is amazing, and the addition of Picodon cheese makes it all the more delectable. You can, if you wish, substitute another goat's cheese that isn't too strong-tasting, and is, above all, well ripened and soft, so that it spreads out in part over the potato as it melts. A green salad would be an ideal accompaniment.

Peel the potatoes, wash them in cold water and pat dry. Using a mandoline, cut the potatoes into julienne and place in a large bowl. Leave for 5 minutes, then squeeze lightly with your hands to remove the water they will have released.

Add the egg, garlic and parsley to the potatoes with a little salt and plenty of pepper, then mix it all together, using your hand or a wooden spoon.

Divide the oil and clarified butter between two 22–24cm non-stick frying pans and place over a medium-high heat until very hot.

Divide the potato mixture between the pans and spread it out evenly using a palette knife, pressing it down so the potato is compact against the base of the pan. Cook for 2–3 minutes until the base has taken on an appealing nut-brown colour, then turn over using a large palette knife and cook on the other side for 3–4 minutes.

Arrange 3 Picodon halves over one of the potato discs, spacing them evenly, then slide the other potato disc on top of this one. Using a palette knife, press the discs together so that they adhere lightly. Arrange the remaining 3 cheese halves on top; these will, with the heat of the potato, melt and spread out over the top.

Slide the crique carefully from the pan onto a rustic board or plate, and serve straight away, cutting it into slices at the table, using a pizza cutter or large, sharp chef's knife.

Croque-monsieur gourmand

SERVES 6

12 slices of sandwich loaf, about 11cm square

1 litre chilled béchamel sauce (see page 246), well seasoned with freshly grated nutmeg, pepper and a touch of cayenne pepper

18 slices of ham, cut to the same size as the bread

120g Aletsch or Gruyère, freshly grated

This is a delicious snack when made with plenty of finely sliced good-quality ham. We serve it at the bar in Le Miedzor, my Swiss alpine restaurant in Crans-Montana; it's always very popular with a glass of local wine. For a light lunch or supper, serve it with a green salad.

Lay a slice of bread on your work surface. Using a palette knife, spread a layer of béchamel over the slice, then place 2 slices of ham on top. Add a second layer of béchamel then place another slice of bread on top, pressing lightly on it. Place another slice of ham on top, then spread a generous layer of béchamel over the ham.

Repeat with the remaining ingredients to make 6 croque-monsieurs in total and place them on a baking tray. Sprinkle the grated cheese over the top of them and press lightly into the béchamel so that it sticks well. Cover the tray with cling film and refrigerate until ready to serve.

Preheat the oven to 180°C/Gas 4. Bake the croque-monsieurs in the oven for 15 minutes. Serve on individual plates, either whole as they are, or cut into triangles.

Pecorino and jalapeño chilli frittata

SERVES 4

75ml light olive oil

1 jalapeño chilli, halved, deseeded and diced

100g spinach leaves, stems removed, well washed and thoroughly drained

1 large tomato, deseeded and diced

12 medium eggs

120g Pecorino Romano, freshly grated

Sea salt and freshly ground pepper

Pecorino Romano DOP (*dénomination d'origine protégée*), which is a hard, pressed sheep's cheese, is particularly good in this frittata, but there are many other cheeses that would work well. For example, I sometimes use Fontina DOP, which is a pressed cow's milk cheese. I like the touch of jalapeño – it complements the spinach, tomato, egg and cheese perfectly. Any leftovers can be eaten cold (but not fridge-cold) the next day – with a slice of toast for breakfast, perhaps.

Heat 2 tbsp of the olive oil in a frying pan over a medium heat, add the chilli and cook for 30 seconds, then add the drained spinach and cook for a further minute. Now add the diced tomato and cook, stirring, for a further 3 minutes. Season lightly with salt.

Tip the mixture into a bowl, or into a colander if necessary to drain off excess liquid; it should be soft but not too wet.

Put the eggs into a bowl, add a little salt and pepper and beat lightly with a fork until evenly combined.

Heat the remaining 3 tbsp oil in a medium frying pan (ideally non-stick) over a high heat. When it is hot, pour in the eggs and cook, stirring with the side of a fork every 20 seconds as you would for an omelette.

As soon as the eggs are barely half-cooked, tip in the spinach mix, spreading it out over the egg, and scatter over the cheese evenly. Lower the heat and stir again for 30 seconds–1 minute. The base of the frittata should now be a light golden colour.

Turn the omelette out onto a lightly oiled flat plate, then slide it back into the frying pan to cook the underside to your liking.

Slide the cooked frittata onto a warmed dish or large plate. Cut the first slice, then let your guests help themselves while it is still hot.

Welsh rarebit

SERVES 5–7

15g butter

15g plain flour

80ml dark beer or stout, ideally Guinness

15g Dijon mustard

A generous pinch of English mustard powder

150g Cheddar, Gloucester or Cheshire (at room temperature), grated

1 small egg, plus an extra yolk

20ml Worcestershire sauce

6–8 drops of Tabasco sauce

A small pinch of cayenne pepper

10 small (10cm) thick-cut slices of white sandwich loaf

10 small cherry tomatoes, halved horizontally

Sea salt and freshly ground pepper

This is a lovely warming snack, best appreciated in winter, around the fire. Some people prefer a milk- rather than beer-based sauce, but I favour the latter as it brings more character and flavour to the dish. An onion and apple chutney is the ideal complement.

Melt the butter in a small saucepan over a low heat, then add the flour and stir with a small balloon whisk. Cook the roux gently for 3–4 minutes, stirring all the time.

Gradually add the beer and bring to the boil, stirring with the whisk. Cook the sauce for 2–3 minutes, stirring constantly, then add both mustards and the grated cheese and cook for a further minute.

Remove from the heat and stir in the whole egg and egg yolk, followed by the Worcestershire sauce, Tabasco and cayenne pepper. Season with salt and pepper to taste.

Preheat a grill and lightly toast the bread slices. Using a palette knife, spread about 50g sauce on each slice of toast. Place under the grill until the sauce turns a dark golden colour.

Transfer the cheese toasts to a board and use a large chef's knife to trim off the crusts, then halve each slice diagonally into 2 triangles.

Serve piping hot on a serving dish or individual plates, arranging the cherry tomatoes around the rarebit. Allow 3 or 4 triangles each.

Chicory and Maroilles cheese tart

SERVES 6

180g chicory bulbs

60g butter, plus extra for greasing

280g flan pastry (see page 249)

Plain flour, for dusting

30g caster sugar

6 juniper berries, crushed with
the flat side of a knife

Juice of ½ lemon

185g ripe Maroilles or Reblochon,
with skin, cut into strips 3–4mm
wide

Sea salt and freshly ground
pepper

This dish, originating in northern France, is simple
and delicious, as long as the pastry base is well cooked,
the cheese is properly ripe and the chicory is cooked to
golden perfection. Reblochon is used in the top tart in the
photograph, Maroilles (which I prefer) in the one below.

Remove the outer layer of leaves from each chicory bulb. Halve
each bulb lengthways, then cut each half into slices.

Lightly butter a loose-based 18cm tart tin, about 3cm high.

Roll out the pastry on a lightly floured surface to a circle, about
3mm thick, giving it a quarter-turn after each roll, and flipping it
over occasionally to stop it sticking and ensure an even thickness.

Loosely roll the pastry around the rolling pin and unfurl it carefully
into the tart tin to line it, pressing the pastry against the side. Roll
the rolling pin across the top of the tin to remove the excess hanging
over the rim. Using floured fingertips, press the pastry against the
inside of the tin, working from the base to the top, to create a small
ridge of pastry, proud of the tin. Place in the fridge to rest.

Heat the butter in a large frying pan over a medium heat. When hot,
add the chicory and dust with the sugar, a pinch of salt and a little
pepper. Add the crushed juniper berries and lemon juice. Cook for
6 minutes, stirring every minute, until lightly caramelised and almost
cooked. Transfer to a colander to drain and cool.

Preheat the oven to 200°C/Gas 6.

Take the chilled tart case out of the fridge and pinch the raised edge
again between your thumb and forefinger, to create a ridge. Prick the
base in 6 or 8 places with a fork. Spread the cooled chicory evenly in
the pastry case and bake in the oven for 20 minutes.

Take out the tart and lower the oven setting to 180°C/Gas 4. Arrange
the cheese slices on top of the chicory and press down lightly, then
return to the oven for a further 20 minutes.

Leave the tart to rest and cool slightly in the tin for 5 minutes before
unmoulding onto a wire rack. Serve warm or at room temperature.

Feta spanakopita

SERVES 6

750g spinach, stems removed,
well washed

6 salad onions, trimmed, white
and green parts thinly sliced

250g feta or kefalotyri cheese,
crumbled

2 medium eggs

20g parsley, leaves only, finely
snipped

10g dill, leaves only, finely snipped

30g Greek black Corinthe
raisins, blanched, refreshed and
thoroughly drained

120ml light olive oil

6 sheets of ready-made filo
pastry, 30 x 18cm

Sea salt and freshly ground
pepper

This spinach and cheese filo pie may be considered ordinary, everyday fare in Greece but I absolutely love it. You can use another crumbly, not-too-rich cheese, such as ricotta or a mild goat's cheese, in place of the feta or kefalotyri, although it won't provide quite the same flavour.

Bring a large pan of water to the boil. Plunge the spinach leaves into the boiling water and blanch for 30 seconds–1 minute, then refresh and drain, squeezing the leaves between your hands to remove as much water as possible. Using a large chef's knife, roughly chop the spinach and set aside in a large bowl.

Preheat the oven to 200°C/Gas 6.

Add the salad onions, cheese and eggs to the spinach and mix with a fork until evenly combined. Add the parsley, dill and raisins and season well with pepper and a little salt, bearing in mind that the cheese is very salty.

Lightly oil a baking tin, about 30 x 20cm, or a 22cm springform cake tin, about 3 or 4cm high. Brush the filo sheets, one at a time, on both sides with the olive oil, then layer them in the tin to line the base and sides, without packing them down; allow to overhang the rim of the tin generously.

Fill the filo pastry case with the spinach mixture, then bring each overhanging filo sheet over the spinach filling, creasing it a little as you do so. Brush olive oil over the top of the creased filo sheets that form the top of the pie, then sprinkle a few drops of water over the filo near the edge of the mould so that they don't burn or colour too much. Bake in the oven for 35–40 minutes.

Leave the pie to rest for 5 minutes before unmoulding. To serve, present the pie whole at the table on a dish or wooden board and cut into slices to serve.

Pain d'épices and cheese millefeuille

SERVES 24

For the tin

50g butter, softened

25g plain flour

For the pain d'épices

300g clear honey

35g butter

1 medium egg

60ml milk

310g 'type 55' plain white flour

8g pain d'épices ground spice mix

2½ tsp bicarbonate of soda

½ tsp sea salt

To assemble

1kg Fourme d'Ambert, thickest part of crust removed

700g softened butter

To serve (optional)

4 ripe pears or a few handfuls of salad leaves

This original snack can be prepared several days in advance. Roquefort, Stilton or any other fairly strong blue cheese can replace the Fourme d'Ambert. You can, of course, choose to fill half of the loaf, which will give you enough for 12 people. You could buy a ready-made pain d'épices, but this home-made version will be far superior. You can find the spice mix in specialist shops. (Also illustrated on previous pages.)

Preheat the oven to 150°C/Gas 2. Butter a 10 x 25cm, 7.5cm deep, loaf tin then sprinkle with the flour and shake out the excess.

In a small saucepan, warm the honey and butter together to about 30°C. Remove from the heat, add the egg and milk and mix using a balloon whisk, without overworking.

Put the flour, spice, bicarbonate of soda and salt into a large bowl. Add the honey mixture and mix with a wooden spoon until smoothly combined. Tip into the prepared tin and bake for 1 hour.

Leave to cool in the tin for about 20 minutes, then carefully turn out and place on a wire rack. Leave to cool completely. Once cooled, wrap the loaf in cling film and refrigerate until ready to use (it will keep well for several days).

Cut the cheese into small pieces and place in a bowl with the softened butter. Mix together, using a large non-flexible whisk.

Using a serrated knife, slice the loaf horizontally into 2–3mm thick slices, starting from the top and working down towards the base. Spread each slice with a thin layer of the cheese and butter mix, then stack in their original order on a small board to re-form the loaf. Holding the loaf between your hands, press down gently but firmly, to bond the slices together with the filling.

Refrigerate the filled loaf for 1–2 hours, then wrap tightly in cling film and keep in the fridge for at least 24 hours, or up to 3 days.

To serve, slice off a crust end, then use a serrated knife to cut the number of slices needed, each about 5mm thick. Offer one slice per serving, as it is or accompanied by a pear quarter, or a few salad leaves.

Salads

Charolais

Valençay

Banon de Provence

Top: Crottin de Chavignol

Tomato and burrata salad with pistou

SERVES 4

1.25kg large tomatoes of different varieties (red, yellow, purple, black etc.)

A handful of baby tomatoes (red or yellow)

1 burrata (about 200g)

100g rocket leaves, tough stems removed, washed and patted dry

3 or 4 basil sprigs

100ml extra virgin olive oil

½ quantity pistou (see page 247)

Sea salt (ideally Guérande) and freshly ground pepper

The success of this dish lies in the selection of tomatoes, which must be perfectly ripe, sweet, juicy and firm. Above all, they should be bursting with flavour and smell strongly of tomato. In the autumn I replace the basil with oregano. If you are unable to find burrata you could use a good buffalo mozzarella instead.

Cut the tomatoes partially or fully into segments or halve them, depending on size; leave baby ones whole. Gently break apart the burrata, revealing the creamy centre.

Scatter the rocket leaves in a shallow serving dish. Arrange the tomatoes and burrata attractively over the rocket. Add the basil leaves and drizzle a few drops of extra virgin olive oil over the salad; serve the rest of the oil separately in a small jug. Spoon a little pistou over the burrata and put the rest into a small bowl.

Sprinkle a little salt and pepper over the salad and serve, letting everyone help themselves to extra olive oil and pistou.

Ilias' Greek salad

SERVES 4

This modern version of Greek salad is full of surprising flavours and textures. It was created by one of my young protégé chefs, Ilias, who is from Greece. Not all of the herbs are essential, just source as many as you can. As a light lunch or a starter, it's a real delight.

250g feta, cut into small pieces

100ml milk

A pinch of cayenne pepper

150g delicate salad leaves, washed and patted dry

12 baby plum or cherry tomatoes, halved crossways

1 small cucumber (about 200g), cut into 3mm slices on an angle

1 medium red onion, finely sliced into rings

12 large caper berries

24 small sprigs of samphire (optional)

20g flat-leaf parsley leaves

10g each of basil, chervil, oregano, marjoram and mint sprigs

10g chives, snipped

For the fried pitta (optional)

3 tbsp olive oil

1 small pitta bread, cut into 4 triangles

For the vinaigrette

6 tbsp olive oil

2 tbsp white wine vinegar

Sea salt and freshly ground pepper

To serve

180g black olive tapenade (see page 248)

If serving the fried pitta, heat the olive oil in a frying pan over a medium heat. Add the pitta triangles and fry lightly until crisp and golden on both sides. Remove to a plate lined with kitchen paper and set aside; keep warm.

For the vinaigrette, in a large salad bowl, whisk the olive oil and wine vinegar together with a pinch each of salt and pepper, using a small balloon whisk.

Put the feta into a small food processor, add the milk and blitz for about 1 minute to a semi-firm mousse consistency. Season with the cayenne pepper; set aside.

Place all of the remaining salad ingredients, including the herbs, in the salad bowl and toss gently to dress with the vinaigrette.

To serve, spoon a portion of tapenade onto each of 4 serving plates and divide the salad between the plates.

Using 2 warmed tablespoons, carefully shape 4 neat quenelles of feta mousse. To do this, take a heaped spoonful of the mousse and pass it repeatedly between the spoons, turning and smoothing the sides as you do so.

Place a feta quenelle on each portion, with a triangle of pitta, if using. Serve immediately.

Green salad with lemony curd dressing

2 Romaine lettuce hearts, or 400g young and tender frisée leaves, or a mixture

50ml grapeseed oil

24 baby capers, drained and blotted dry

2 lemons

20 tarragon leaves (preferably) or chervil sprigs

For the dressing

200ml curdled milk (see note)

Juice of 1 lemon

Sea salt and freshly ground pepper

My mother used to curdle milk for us, using a little lemon juice or vinegar, to achieve the consistency of semi-set yoghurt before you could even buy pots of yoghurt. It makes a beautifully natural and clean-tasting dressing for salad leaves, especially when very lemony, as it is here.

Pick over the salad leaves, wash in cold water, drain and dry well.

Heat the oil in a small pan to about 160°C, add the capers and fry for 1–2 minutes until crisp, then remove with a slotted spoon and dry on kitchen paper.

Using a sharp, flexible-bladed knife, cut off the skin, pith and outer membranes from the whole lemons, then release the segments by sliding the blade in between the membranes. Set aside in a bowl.

For the dressing, mix the curdled milk and lemon juice together in a salad bowl and season with some salt and pepper.

Add the salad leaves to the dressing and toss gently, then add the lemon segments and sprinkle with the tarragon or chervil. Serve the fried capers in a separate bowl, for everyone to help themselves.

To curdle milk, gently warm 250ml milk in a small pan over a medium heat until just steaming, then stir in 1 tbsp lemon juice. Take off the heat and leave to stand for 10 minutes to allow the curds to form, then drain in a muslin-lined sieve.

Savoy cabbage salad with Tilsit cheese

SERVES 4

1 firm, small Savoy or Chinese cabbage (about 400g)

80ml groundnut oil

2½ tbsp cider vinegar (ideally) or white wine vinegar

10g caraway seeds

180g Tilsit cheese

2 whole hot-smoked trout

1 red pepper, halved, cored and deseeded

2 apples, preferably Cox

Juice of ½ lemon

15g flat-leaf parsley leaves

Sea salt and freshly ground pepper

I love the marriage of raw tender cabbage with apple and smoked trout. The red pepper lends a touch of colour and the cheese adds another dimension to this autumnal/wintry salad. Tilsit is a semi-hard cow's cheese that takes its name from the Prussian town of Tilsit (today called Sovetsk, in Russia) where it originated. It is popular in Switzerland, too. The flavour can be mild and light but also sometimes gently salty, which I prefer. If you cannot find it, use Gouda instead.

Remove the outer leaves from the cabbage, then halve lengthways and slice each cabbage half as finely as possible. Place in a large bowl. Add the oil, vinegar and a little salt and pepper. Scatter over the caraway seeds, toss well and set aside for at least 20 minutes.

Cut the cheese into cubes or batons. Remove the skin from the smoked trout, lift off the 4 fillets and set aside on a plate. Cut the red pepper into fine julienne. Peel, core and roughly chop the apples, then sprinkle with lemon juice to prevent discoloration.

To serve, add the red pepper julienne and chopped apple to the cabbage, toss to combine and check for seasoning.

Divide the salad between 4 plates, piling it into a neat mound, then flake a trout fillet over each mound. Scatter over the cheese cubes and a few parsley leaves to serve.

Watercress and Rogue River blue cheese salad

SERVES 4

12 walnut halves

100ml cold milk

1 ripe pomegranate (optional)

1 ripe, juicy pear

Juice of ½ lemon

About 250g watercress, stems removed, washed and patted dry

160g Rogue River blue cheese, cut into small pieces

For the dressing

8 tsp grapeseed oil

4 tsp white wine vinegar

Sea salt and freshly ground pepper

Rogue River, which is made in Oregon in the United States was the first blue-veined raw cow's milk cheese to be certified for export, a decade ago. Wrapped in vine leaves, it has a distinctive, but not overpowering, flavour and a delightful creamy texture. It is divine, especially when eaten with pears and walnuts. Another lightly marbled blue cheese, such as Bleu de Bresse, can be used in place of Rogue River, but the salad won't have quite the same character.

Drop the walnut halves, a few at a time, into a small pan of simmering water for 2 minutes, then remove and gently peel them, using the tip of the knife. Immerse in the cold milk to soak.

Halve the pomegranate, if using, and remove the red seeds, avoiding the bitter membrane. Set aside in a bowl.

Peel, halve and core the pear, then cut into cubes. Place in a bowl and spritz with the lemon juice to stop the flesh discolouring.

For the dressing, put the oil and wine vinegar into a salad bowl with a pinch each of salt and pepper and whisk to combine.

Drain the walnuts and pat dry. Add the watercress to the vinaigrette and mix gently, then add the walnuts, pomegranate seeds, if using, and the cubes of pear. Mix the salad lightly, then scatter over the cheese to serve.

Salad of grilled treviso, watermelon and smoked cheese

SERVES 4

2 treviso (or ordinary radicchio)

300g piece of ripe, firm-fleshed watermelon

1 large red onion, halved lengthways and cut into thick wedges

100ml light, fruity olive oil

1 tbsp balsamic vinegar

120g smoked Scamorza cheese, cut into 4 slices about 1cm thick

2 tbsp clear honey

Sea salt and freshly ground pepper

1 lemon, cut into 8 wedges, to serve

I adore this colourful, rustic salad, which is bursting with flavours. There is a hint of bitterness from the treviso (the long-leafed variety of radicchio), sweetness from the watermelon and a mild sharpness from the red onion. Balsamic vinegar, mingled with honey and fruity olive oil, bring it all together. Other smoked cheeses can be used in place of Scamorza, such as Calumet, Golden Rebel or smoked Gouda.

Remove the outermost 2 or 3 leaves from each treviso (or other radicchio), then halve lengthways and cut each half into 2 or 3 long wedges. Rinse in cold water, without separating out the leaves. Drain and dry well.

Deseed the watermelon and cut away the hard peel and white part next to the skin. Cut the watermelon into 4 large pieces.

Preheat a large griddle pan (or barbecue).

Brush the pieces of watermelon, onion and treviso with a little olive oil. Lightly oil the ridges of the griddle pan (or barbecue grid).

Arrange the watermelon, onion and treviso in the pan (or on the barbecue). Leave for about 30 seconds, then give each piece a quarter-turn and cook for another 30 seconds. Now flip them all over and repeat as for the first side, leaving the treviso for an extra 30 seconds.

Transfer the watermelon, onion and treviso to a large, shallow serving dish and toss gently to combine. Drizzle the remaining olive oil over the treviso, followed by the balsamic vinegar, sprinkling a few drops of vinegar over the watermelon as well. Add a light sprinkling of salt and a generous grinding of pepper to the salad.

Grill the smoked cheese for 30–45 seconds in the griddle pan or on the barbecue, then add to the salad. Immediately drizzle the honey over everything. Serve at once, with the lemon wedges on the side.

Caesar salad

1 small smoked duck breast, very finely sliced, or 120g finely sliced pancetta

2 slices of white sandwich loaf

6 anchovy fillets in olive oil, halved lengthways

1 Romaine lettuce, outer leaves removed, washed and patted dry

100g Parmigiano Reggiano, freshly shaved

Sea salt and freshly ground pepper

For the Caesar dressing

1 egg yolk (use pasteurised if keeping for 2 days)

1½ tsp Dijon mustard

1 small garlic clove, chopped

100ml light olive oil

25g Parmigiano Reggiano, freshly grated

2 anchovy fillets in olive oil, cut into diced

3g tarragon leaves, snipped

Juice of 1 lemon

The origins of this salad date back to the 1920s – to Mexico and the United States, and to restaurateur Caesar Cardini. Some people prepare it with lobster or chicken, but I prefer it with crisp pancetta, or a lightly smoked duck breast. It is a delicious salad but can have the misfortune of being loosely interpreted by charlatans, which ruins the final result…

First prepare the Caesar dressing. In a medium bowl, mix the egg yolk, mustard and garlic to combine, then add the olive oil, a little at a time, mixing with a hand-held stick blender to a homogeneous, creamy sauce.

Incorporate the grated cheese, anchovies, tarragon and lemon juice and season with salt and pepper to taste. If the dressing seems too thick, add a trickle of lukewarm water.

If using smoked duck breast, have ready at room temperature. If using pancetta, preheat the oven to 160°C/Gas 3. Place the pancetta slices between 2 sheets of silicone paper on a baking sheet. Place another baking sheet on top, to weigh down. Bake for 20 minutes, then remove and set aside.

Toast the bread slices, remove the crusts, then cut into batons. Wrap the halved anchovy fillets decoratively around the toasted batons.

To serve, gently toss the Romaine leaves with the Caesar dressing, then divide between 4 plates, mounding the leaves up slightly. Arrange the smoked duck breast or crisp pancetta slices and the anchovy-wrapped batons on top. Scatter the Parmesan shavings over the salad and serve.

Lamb's lettuce, artichoke and cottage cheese salad

1 tender, freshly picked corn-on-the-cob, outer husk removed

400g lamb's lettuce

6 small (poivrade) artichokes

Juice of 1 lemon

24 hazelnuts (ideally fresh) or cobnuts

About 160g cottage cheese

A pinch of ground Espelette pepper

A few young, tender tarragon leaves, or a few chives, snipped

For the dressing

4 tbsp light olive or hazelnut oil

4 tsp red wine vinegar

Sea salt and freshly ground pepper

This is a lovely salad to prepare when young artichokes are in season. It's particularly delicious with fresh hazelnuts – or cobnuts – but the more familiar dried hazelnuts are suitable. You can also use ricotta in place of cottage cheese.

Add the corn cob to a pan of boiling salted water and cook for 5–15 minutes until tender (very fresh and/early season corn takes little time). Drain and refresh in cold water then lift onto a board. Using a sharp knife, slice down the cob to remove the corn kernels. Put these into a bowl, cover with cling film and set aside.

Using a small knife, trim off the very end of the base of each little sprig of lamb's lettuce and place in a bowl of ice-cold water to crisp up. After 15 minutes, change the water for ice-cold again, then after 15 minutes drain the salad, dry and set aside in the fridge.

Remove the outer, tougher darker leaves from each artichoke, by twisting and pulling them off. Using a small, sharp knife, cut the top off each artichoke then, using a teaspoon or melon baller, scoop out the choke from the centre. Trim the bases and pare off a little of the stalk, to remove the greener and less tender areas. Cut off all but about 3cm of the stalk. Cut each artichoke into quarters, rinse in cold water and place in a bowl. Spritz with the lemon juice and turn the artichokes in the juice to prevent discoloration.

To prepare the dressing, whisk the oil and wine vinegar together in a large bowl using a small balloon whisk and season with a little salt and pepper.

Add the lamb's lettuce to the dressing and toss gently to coat. Divide between 4 plates and arrange the artichoke quarters on top. Scatter over the hazelnuts and corn kernels.

Finally, using 2 dessertspoons, shape quenelles of cottage cheese. To do this, take a heaped spoonful of cottage cheese and pass it repeatedly between the spoons, turning and smoothing the sides as you do so. Place 3 quenelles on each portion of salad, dust with Espelette pepper, sprinkle with the tarragon or chives and serve.

Beetroot salad with goat's cheese

SERVES 4

250g lamb's lettuce

10–12 fresh walnuts in shells (ideally), or 24 dried walnut halves

200ml cold milk (if using dried nuts)

2 beetroot, cooked with skins on, (about 300g in total)

1 crisp apple, such as Granny Smith

Juice of ½ lemon

120g ash-coated goat's cheese (see note)

For the vinaigrette dressing

4 tbsp walnut oil (or 2 tbsp each walnut and groundnut oil for a milder flavour)

2 tbsp red wine vinegar

Sea salt and freshly ground pepper

Some fresh goat's cheeses are coated in ash to reduce the acidity on the surface of the cheese and encourage the rind to form. Typically these cheeses are soft, beautifully smooth and flavoursome, without being too strong.

Beetroot marries beautifully with goat's cheese, walnuts, apple and tender lamb's lettuce in this autumnal salad. Whenever I can, I buy raw beetroot from the market and cook them in salted water then dry them out (skins on), on a bed of salt in the oven preheated to 160°C/Gas 3 for about 30 minutes. They are far more flavourful than beetroot sold pre-cooked.

Using a small knife, trim off the very end of the base of each little sprig of lamb's lettuce and place in a bowl of ice-cold water to crisp up. After 15 minutes, change the water for ice-cold again, then after 15 minutes drain the salad, dry and set aside in the fridge.

If using fresh walnuts, carefully break open (without damaging them) and take out the nut halves; set aside. If using dried walnuts, in 2 batches, plunge into boiling water for 2 minutes, then peel away the skins using the tip of a small knife, without breaking the nuts. Once peeled, immerse in the cold milk for at least 20 minutes. Just before serving, drain and pat dry with kitchen paper.

Peel the beetroot and cut the wide part in the middle horizontally into very fine slices, as for a carpaccio. Cut the end pieces into evenly sized small dice.

Rinse the apple in cold water and dry it, then, using a mandoline (ideally fitted with the waffle cutter), cut thin slices from the apple, giving the apple a quarter-turn between each and stopping before the core. Sprinkle with lemon juice to prevent discoloration.

For the dressing, whisk the walnut oil and wine vinegar together in a bowl and season with salt and pepper to taste. Add the lamb's lettuce and toss gently to coat in the vinaigrette.

To serve, divide the sliced beetroot between 4 serving plates, then add 4 apple (waffle) slices to each, and the diced beetroot in little heaps in between the apple. Place slices of goat's cheese on the apple waffle slices then top with the walnut halves. Finally, arrange the lamb's lettuce in a neat pile in the middle of each plate.

Puy lentil, cherry tomato and goat's cheese salad

SERVES 6

180g green Puy lentils

1 medium carrot, cut into large dice

1 bouquet garni (a few thyme sprigs, a bay leaf and a small handful of parsley stalks, tied together)

1 medium onion (ideally red), finely diced

100ml light olive oil

2 tbsp red wine vinegar

A pinch of cayenne pepper

½ celeriac, peeled, cut into julienne

Juice of ½ lemon

3 small semi-fresh goat's cheeses, each cut into 6 pieces

6 slices of baguette (cut 5mm thick on the diagonal)

12 cherry tomatoes, halved

A few coriander leaves, finely snipped

Sea salt and freshly ground pepper

I love this salad with its contrasting textures and flavours: crisp celeriac julienne, soft lentils, juicy tomatoes, flavourful goat's cheese and onion. The components can be prepared in advance, ready to assemble a few minutes before serving.

Put the lentils into a pan and cover generously with cold water. Bring to the boil over a medium heat and cook for 2 minutes, then skim off any impurities from the surface and tip the lentils into a colander to drain.

Return the lentils to the pan and cover generously again with cold water. Add the carrot, bouquet garni and a pinch of salt. Bring to the boil, lower the heat and cook at a gentle simmer for 20–25 minutes until tender. Remove from the heat and leave to cool in the cooking water until barely warm.

Pick out and discard the bouquet garni, drain the lentils and carrot well and transfer to a salad bowl. Add the diced onion and trickle over the olive oil and wine vinegar. Season with the cayenne and a little salt and pepper, then toss everything together. Leave to stand for 10–15 minutes.

Meanwhile, peel the celeriac and cut into julienne. Add to a pan of boiling water and blanch for 30 seconds, then drain and refresh in cold water. Drain thoroughly and tip into a bowl. Add the lemon juice and toss well.

Just before serving, add the celeriac julienne to the lentil salad, followed by the pieces of goat's cheese. Rub the baguette slices very lightly with the cherry tomato halves and sprinkle the coriander over them. Gently mix the tomato halves into the lentils, arrange the baguette slices around the edge of the bowl and serve.

Rice salad with Comté cheese

SERVES 4

200g long-grain rice

2 generous pinches of mild curry powder

6 tbsp light olive oil

3 tbsp white wine vinegar

30g pine nuts

160g Comté (aged for 6–8 months)

½ bunch of radishes, ideally pink, trimmed and quartered lengthways

30g sultanas, blanched and drained

Sea salt and freshly ground pepper

This simple salad is surprisingly good. A little curry powder added to rice at the end of cooking lends colour and a subtle flavour. The creamy texture and fruity notes of a Comté aged for 6–8 months work in perfect harmony with the sweetness of the sultanas and crunch of radish. You could use another firm cheese such as Pavé du Nord in place of the Comté, but as it is stronger it would be better to cut this into slivers or shavings rather than dice.

Bring a large pan of water to the boil, shower in the rice and cook over a low heat for about 18 minutes until the grains are *al dente* (cooked but firm to the bite) and no longer crunchy. Remove from the heat and add the curry powder with a pinch of salt.

Leave the rice in the cooking water for 1–2 minutes, stirring once or twice, then drain in a fine sieve. Rinse the rice under the cold tap, just to cool it slightly. Drain well.

Put the olive oil, wine vinegar and a pinch each of salt and pepper into a large salad bowl and whisk with a balloon whisk. Add the drained rice and toss to mix with the vinaigrette, then cover with cling film and set aside.

Toast the pine nuts on a baking tray in an oven preheated to 180°C/ Gas 4 for 5–8 minutes or in a dry frying pan, shaking frequently, for about 3 minutes until lightly coloured. Tip into a cup and set aside.

Remove the rind from the Comté and cut into small dice.

Gently mix the radishes, sultanas and cheese through the rice. Taste and adjust the seasoning with salt and pepper as required, then scatter over the toasted pine nuts to serve.

New potato salad with anchovy, egg and grilled smoked cheese

SERVES 4

600g small new potatoes, washed

8 anchovy fillets in oil, well drained

4 slices of smoked Scamorza cheese, about 1cm thick

A little light olive oil, for oiling

2 hard-boiled eggs, peeled and cut in half lengthways

8 green olives

1 bunch of chives, cut into short lengths

A handful of small oregano sprigs

Sea salt and freshly ground pepper

For the mayonnaise

2 egg yolks

2 tsp Dijon mustard

80ml light olive oil

4 tsp white wine vinegar

This is a delicious salad where all the ingredients go together wonderfully. Scamorza, as with all smoked cheeses, only tastes good grilled when still hot or warm, or it will turn rubbery. Yorkshire Wensleydale, Irish Ardsallagh or Gouda, all in their smoked versions, can be substituted for Scamorza.

Add the potatoes to a pan of salted water, bring to the boil and cook in their skins until just tender. Drain and leave until cool enough to handle, then peel away the skins with a small knife. Halve any larger potatoes, leave small ones whole.

To make the mayonnaise, put the egg yolks into a bowl with the mustard and a little salt and pepper and mix together using a small balloon whisk. Incorporate the olive oil a little at a time in a thin trickle, stirring constantly with the whisk. As soon as it is all incorporated, add the wine vinegar and season to taste with salt and a generous grinding of pepper. The mayonnaise should be not too stiff; add a few drops of warm water to let it down if necessary.

Preheat a griddle pan (or grill or barbecue).

Put the cooked potatoes into a large bowl with the anchovy fillets. Add the mayonnaise and mix gently, using a spatula.

Just before serving, very lightly oil the slices of Scamorza then griddle (or grill or barbecue) for 20 seconds on each side, using your chosen method. Set aside on a warmed plate.

To serve, tip the potato salad into a large, shallow serving dish and add the hard-boiled egg halves. Scatter the olives on top of the salad and sprinkle over the chives and oregano. Arrange the just-grilled, hot slices of Scarmorza around the edge of the dish and serve at once.

Fish & Shellfish

Parmigiano Reggiano

Langoustine with 'fritot' and Manchego

SERVES 2

4–6 raw langoustines, depending on size

100ml light olive oil

1 medium onion, chopped

1 red or green pepper, halved, cored, deseeded and cut into large strips

140g tomatoes, peeled, deseeded and diced

1 garlic clove, chopped

A knifetip of cayenne pepper

70ml water

120g Manchego, cut into large dice

Sea salt

A small handful of coriander leaves, to finish

I adore this dish, with its Spanish aromas. The succulent langoustines sit on a bed of flavourful *fritot* (a regional ragout of vegetables from the south of Spain, typically made with tomatoes and peppers), dotted with semi-melted pieces of Manchego. Bread is essential, to mop up all the tasty juices. You could use another semi-hard cheese, such as Gruyère, in place of the Manchego but it won't quite match it.

Bring a large pan of lightly salted water to the boil. As soon as it boils, drop in the langoustines and blanch at a gentle simmer for 2 minutes. Drain and drop into a bowl of cold water with a few ice cubes added. Leave for 5 minutes, then drain and place in a bowl. Cover with a damp tea towel and set aside.

Heat 50ml of the olive oil in a sauté pan over a medium heat. Add the onion and pepper and sauté for 2 minutes, then add the tomatoes and garlic and simmer over a gentle heat for 20 minutes, stirring every 5 minutes. Set the *fritot* aside; keep warm.

Detach the langoustine heads from their tails. Keep the two nicest looking heads with their pincers for serving. Using the flat of a large knife, crush the other heads and carefully peel the tails, which should be only lightly cooked.

Heat 2 tbsp olive oil in a frying pan over a medium heat. Sprinkle the cayenne and some salt over the langoustine tails. When the oil is hot, add them to the pan and colour for 1 minute, turning occasionally. Remove from the pan and add to the *fritot*.

Add the crushed langoustine heads to the pan and colour for 3–4 minutes, then pour on the 70ml water and cook over a low heat for 2–3 minutes. Strain the liquor through a chinois into the *fritot*.

Heat the *fritot* in its sauté pan over a gentle heat for 2–3 minutes, stirring to incorporate the liquor. Add the Manchego and stir gently.

Tip the contents of the sauté pan into a warmed shallow serving dish, bringing the langoustine tails to the surface. Arrange the reserved langoustine heads on the edge of the dish and brush them with the remaining olive oil. Scatter over the coriander leaves and serve straight away.

Lobster gratin

Serves 6 as a starter,
3 as a main course

This is a real feast for the palate. You can buy lobster ready-cooked, but the flavours will not be as distinct or delicate.

3 lobsters (about 400–500g each), ideally live and placed in the freezer for 20 minutes to sedate before cooking

1 leek, washed and finely sliced

1 lemon, cut into quarters

10g coarse salt

For the sauce

40g very finely chopped shallot

200ml fish stock (see page 244)

200ml dry white wine

300ml béchamel sauce (see page 246)

100ml double cream

2 tsp Dijon mustard

1 tsp English mustard powder, mixed with a few drops of water

50g chilled butter, cut into small dice

A pinch of cayenne pepper

40g Parmigiano Reggiano, freshly grated

Sea salt

To finish

40g dried breadcrumbs (ideally panko)

40g Parmigiano Reggiano, freshly grated

12 semi-confit cherry tomatoes (see page 248), warmed

Fill a pan large enough to take the 3 lobsters with cold water. Add the leek, lemon and salt and bring to the boil. Lower the lobsters into the water and cook at a very gentle simmer for 15 minutes. Using a skimmer, lift the lobsters onto a wire rack and leave to cool.

For the sauce, put the shallot, fish stock and wine into a saucepan, bring to the boil over a medium heat and reduce by two-thirds. Add the béchamel and cook over a low heat for 25 minutes, stirring occasionally with a whisk. Add the cream, simmer for 5 minutes, then add both mustards and cook for another 2 minutes. Remove from the heat and whisk in the butter, a little at a time, then add the cayenne. Add a little salt, then shower in the Parmesan, stirring with a whisk. Cover and set aside. Preheat the oven to 180°C/Gas 4.

Break off the large claws from the lobsters and set aside, then split each tail in half down the middle, using a large chef's knife, from head to tail. Take out the meat from the halved shells and remove and discard the digestive tract that runs the length of each tail. Cut the tail meat into 3 medallions (to give 6 pieces) and set aside.

Remove the green gland and coral from the lobster heads. Rinse the shells in cold water and dry well. Break open the claws in 2 or 3 places, using the back of a large, heavy knife, then prise out the claw meat, without breaking it. Set aside with the tail medallions.

Place the 6 empty half shells on a baking tray. Brush the insides of each with a little of the sauce, then arrange 3 lobster medallion pieces, dipped lightly in the sauce, in each half shell, and some claw meat in each head shell. Spoon the rest of the sauce over the meat. Mix the breadcrumbs with the Parmesan and sprinkle evenly on top.

Place in the oven for 15 minutes, to heat through and colour the surface a little. If necessary, place under a hot grill for 1–2 minutes to achieve the colour.

Arrange the warm cherry tomatoes in the head, near the claw meat, and serve one lobster half per guest for a starter, or a couple of halves for a main course.

Gratin of mussels on pilaf rice

SERVES 4

1.5–2kg large live mussels

60g butter

3 shallots, finely chopped

150g long-grain rice

300ml boiling water, lightly salted

2 small bouquets garnis (thyme sprig, bay leaf and a few parsley stalks, tied together)

½ red pepper, cored and deseeded

50ml dry white wine

300ml double cream

50g Stilton, crushed with a fork

30g white breadcrumbs

Sea salt and freshly ground pepper

This is a delightful dish to serve in autumn or winter, when mussels are at their best. The Stilton can be replaced with another blue cheese, such as a Bleu d'Auvergne or Saint-Agur.

Scrub the mussels clean and de-beard if necessary, using the back of a small knife. Rinse thoroughly in cold water. Drain well.

Melt the butter in a heavy-based saucepan over a medium heat. Add one-third of the shallots and cook, stirring, for 1 minute, then shower in the rice and cook, stirring, for 2–3 minutes. Add the water and a bouquet garni. Cover and cook over a low heat for 18 minutes.

Cut the red pepper into small diamonds and blanch in boiling water for 1 minute, then drain and fork through the rice. Keep warm.

Put the wine, remaining shallots and second bouquet garni in a large pan and place over a high heat. As soon as it boils, add the mussels and cover with a tight-fitting lid. Cook, stirring every 2 minutes until the mussels have opened. Take off the heat and leave to stand for 3–4 minutes. Strain the juices through a fine sieve into a bowl.

Remove the mussels from their shells and add to the juices in the bowl. Set aside the most attractive half of each shell for serving.

Tip the mussel juices into a pan; keep the mussels in the bowl, covered with cling film. Let the juices bubble over a high heat to reduce by one-quarter. In another pan, reduce the cream over a medium heat by one-third, then add the reduced mussel juices. Leave to simmer and reduce until the sauce is thick enough to coat the back of a spoon. Remove from the heat, whisk in the crushed Stilton and season with pepper, and a little salt if needed.

Preheat the grill to high. Place the empty reserved shells in a shallow dish. Add a mussel or two to each, depending on the size of the shell. Carefully and generously spoon the sauce over the mussels to cover them well, then sprinkle with the breadcrumbs. Place under the hot grill for 2 or 3 minutes to colour lightly.

To serve, remove the bouquet garni from the rice, then divide between warmed shallow bowls. Arrange the mussels on the rice, keeping them close together. Serve at once.

Sardine paupiettes

Serves 6 as a starter,
3 as a main course

6 sardines (about 100g each)

150g Brin d'Amour or other ewe's milk cheese, or semi-soft goat's cheese

1 small egg

1 tbsp snipped chives

1 small garlic clove, finely chopped

1 tbsp white breadcrumbs

1 lemon, finely sliced

70ml mild olive oil

20g baby capers, rinsed and well drained

2 or 3 sprigs each of oregano and marjoram

Freshly ground pepper

Ground Espelette pepper, to finish

For this dish the sardines need to be fairly large to hold the tasty stuffing. Depending on their size, one sardine will be adequate as a starter, or you can serve two per person as a main dish. Brin d'Amour is a semi-soft Corsican ewe's milk cheese with a distinctive flavour. It can be replaced with any Corsican brocciu, or a goat's cheese with character, such as Charolais, or Golden Cross from East Sussex.

Gently remove the scales from the sardines using your thumbnail then cut off the heads and slit open the bellies, keeping the tails on. Remove the guts with your thumb, then carefully pull out the central backbone with your fingers, or prise it out using a small knife if necessary. Wipe each sardine gently with a damp tea towel or kitchen paper; do not wash them. Lay out on a work surface, flesh side up, sprinkle with pepper and cover with cling film.

Put the cheese into a bowl and crush with a fork, then add the egg, chives, garlic, breadcrumbs and some pepper. Mix well with the fork until well combined and the consistency required for a stuffing.

Preheat the oven to 180°C/Gas 4.

Using 2 warmed tablespoons, carefully shape a neat quenelle of stuffing. To do this, take a heaped spoonful of the stuffing and pass it repeatedly between the spoons, turning and smoothing the sides as you do so. Place on one side of each butterflied sardine and bring the other side over to enclose. Secure the opening with a bamboo skewer or two, taking care not to damage the delicate flesh. Repeat with the remaining 5 sardines and stuffing mixture.

Line the base of an ovenproof dish with the lemon slices, trickle over a little of the olive oil, then arrange the sardines, side by side, in a single layer on top. Brush with the remaining olive oil, scatter over the capers and cook in the oven, uncovered, for 4 minutes. Take the dish out and add the herb sprigs, then cover with foil and return to the oven for 1½–2 minutes, no longer.

Serve at once, encouraging everyone to help themselves to the fish and spooning over some of the juices released during cooking. Serve some Espelette pepper separately in a small dish, for anyone who wishes to add a pinch of extra spice to their fish.

Sea bass with a Parmesan crumb coating and aubergine 'caviar'

4 fairly thick fillets of sea bass (about 180g each), skin on

2 medium eggs

40ml light olive oil, plus 3 tbsp for the coating

80g Parmigiano Reggiano, freshly grated

40g dried breadcrumbs (ideally panko)

100g butter, diced

For the aubergine 'caviar'

2 firm, medium aubergines, stalk end trimmed

110ml light olive oil

1 garlic clove, finely chopped

2 sprigs of thyme

2 bay leaves, snipped into small pieces

6 basil leaves, finely snipped

Sea salt and freshly ground pepper

To serve

1 lemon, cut into 4 wedges

8 small basil leaves

This crisp Parmesan crumb coating is a lovely foil for the succulent sea bass, and the aubergine complements this light and flavoursome fish perfectly.

Preheat the oven to 180°C/Gas 4.

For the 'caviar', halve each aubergine lengthways. Cut a long, thin (2mm) slice from the cut side of each half, wrap in cling film and place in the fridge. Using a sharp knife, mark a cross-hatch pattern, 5mm deep, in the cut surface of the aubergine halves. Brush with 50ml olive oil and scatter evenly with the garlic, thyme and bay. Sprinkle with salt and pepper. Wrap each aubergine half in foil, place on a baking tray and bake for 25–30 minutes.

Take the aubergines from the oven and remove the foil, being careful as they will be very hot. Using a spoon, scrape off the aromatics, then scoop the aubergine flesh onto a board, scraping the skins lightly to remove all the flesh. Discard the skins.

Using a large chef's knife, chop the aubergine flesh almost to a purée, then transfer to a saucepan and place over a low heat. Add 30ml olive oil and the snipped basil. Season to taste with salt and pepper. As soon as it starts to bubble, remove from the heat. Keep warm, covered with cling film pierced in several places.

Heat the remaining 30ml olive oil in a frying pan over a medium heat. Add the reserved aubergine slices and cook for 1–2 minutes on each side, until lightly golden. Set aside on kitchen paper.

For the fish, in a shallow dish, beat the eggs, 3 tbsp olive oil and a little salt and pepper together using a fork. Mix the Parmesan and breadcrumbs together on another plate. Pat the fish dry with kitchen paper and dip, one at a time, into the beaten egg and then into the crumb mixture, pressing this on so it sticks to the fish.

continued overleaf

continued from previous page

To cook the fish, heat the 40ml olive oil with the butter in a large frying pan over a medium heat. When it is hot, add the coated fish pieces in a single layer and cook for 2½–3 minutes. Turn and cook on the other side for a further 2½–3 minutes, basting once or twice. Remove from the pan and drain on kitchen paper.

While the fish is cooking, place a 5–6cm plain cutter on a warmed serving plate. Line the inside of the ring with one of the cooked aubergine slices then two-thirds fill with the aubergine 'caviar'. Carefully lift off the cutter, turning it slightly to help detach it. Repeat with the remaining aubergine slices and 'caviar' on the other 3 warmed plates.

Place a sea bass fillet on each plate and add a lemon quarter. Slot 2 basil leaves into the top of each aubergine caviar and serve, trickled with any juices from the aubergine 'caviar'.

Smoked salmon on cucumber julienne with a Mornay glaze

SERVES 4

1 medium cucumber (about 180g)

200ml dry white wine

1 small shallot, finely chopped

1 thyme sprig, leaves stripped

60g butter, cut into small pieces

½ quantity Mornay sauce (see page 246)

A pinch of cayenne pepper

20g dill, leaves picked

8 fine slices of smoked salmon (about 60g each, 480g in total)

30g Parmigiano Reggiano, freshly grated

Sea salt and freshly ground pepper

This is a delicious, elegant dish that is quick to prepare and a treat for the palate. Another cheese, such as Fontina DOP, can be substituted for the Parmesan but won't deliver quite the same finesse.

Using a swivel vegetable peeler, peel the cucumber and halve it lengthways, then scoop out the seeds using a teaspoon. Cut the flesh into fine julienne with a mandoline or large chef's knife and place in a bowl; set aside.

Put the wine, shallot and thyme leaves into a small pan and let bubble over a medium heat to reduce by three-quarters. Remove from the heat and, using a small balloon whisk, incorporate the butter a few pieces at a time, whisking constantly. Season with salt and a generous grinding of pepper. Set this beurre blanc aside.

Gently heat the Mornay sauce until it reaches 80–90°C, then set aside; keep hot.

When ready to serve, preheat the grill and warm 4 large, shallow serving plates.

Mix the cucumber julienne into the beurre blanc. Add the cayenne pepper and one-third of the dill, finely snipped, and heat through very lightly.

Divide the cucumber between the warmed plates and place 2 slices of smoked salmon on each serving. Coat with the Mornay sauce and sprinkle the Parmesan over the top. Place under the grill for a minute or two – just long enough to give it a light golden glaze. Garnish with the remaining dill and serve at once.

Flaked cod on a bed of spinach with grilled goat's cheese

SERVES 4

1 leek, white part only, well washed and finely sliced

2–3 thyme sprigs, leaves stripped, stems reserved

2 bay leaves

½ lemon, cut into 4 pieces

100ml dry white wine

400g middle fillet of cod, cut into 8 large cubes

90g butter

350g leaf spinach, well washed and stems removed

1 semi-firm goat's cheese log, cut into 8 rounds about 1cm thick

1 tbsp light olive oil

30ml double cream

Sea salt and freshly ground pepper

The simplest of fish dishes, this is light and wonderfully flavourful. To complement the unadorned fish, the goat's cheese needs to be fairly fresh with a mild, gentle flavour, rather than fully ripened. (Illustrated on previous page.)

Fill a shallow pan with cold water, add the leek, thyme stems, bay leaves, lemon, wine and a small pinch of salt. Bring to a simmer and let bubble for 10 minutes, then add the cubes of cod, put the lid on and take the pan off the heat. Set aside to allow the cod to cook in the residual heat.

Strain two-thirds of the cod poaching liquor into another pan and let bubble to reduce by two-thirds. Remove from the heat and set aside.

Meanwhile, heat 30g of the butter in a large frying pan over a medium heat. Add half the spinach leaves, season very lightly with salt and cook for 1½ minutes, stirring every 30 seconds, then tip into a colander to drain. Cook the remaining spinach in the same way using another 30g butter, adding it to the cooked spinach in the colander once done.

Preheat the grill to high. Place the goat's cheese rounds on a very lightly oiled small baking tray, sprinkle over the reserved thyme leaves and drizzle with a little olive oil. Place under the grill for 1–2 minutes until lightly coloured.

Add the cream to the reduced poaching liquor. Bring to the boil and let bubble gently for 1–2 minutes, then whisk in the remaining 30g butter, a small piece at a time. Add a little salt and pepper to taste. Set this beurre blanc aside; keep hot.

To serve, divide the drained spinach between 4 warmed serving plates. Drain the cubes of cod and flake two over each plate of spinach, by gently pressing the cubes between your thumb and forefinger. Arrange 2 grilled goat's cheese rounds on each plate and spoon the beurre blanc around the edge. Serve at once.

Grilled halibut steak with Parmesan and ginger hollandaise

SERVES 4

4 halibut steaks (about 220g each)

60ml light olive or grapeseed oil

20g Parmigiano Reggiano, freshly grated

Sea salt and freshly ground pepper

For the Parmesan and ginger hollandaise

2 tbsp cold water

1½ tbsp white wine vinegar

1 tsp roughly crushed black pepper

3 egg yolks

200g clarified butter

30g Parmigiano Reggiano, freshly grated

Juice of ½ lemon

5g fresh ginger, peeled and finely grated

To serve

1 lemon, quartered

The success of this simple dish lies in the grilling of the fish, which must not be overdone, and in the sauce, with its hints of Parmesan and ginger. Serve some simply boiled French beans or wilted spinach on the side.

First make the hollandaise. Put the water, wine vinegar and crushed pepper into a small pan, place over a low heat and let bubble gently to reduce by one-third. Remove from the heat and leave to cool.

Meanwhile, heat a ridged griddle pan over a medium heat.

Once the reduced liquor is cold, add the egg yolks and mix, using a small balloon whisk. Place the pan over a gentle heat (use a heat diffuser if you have one) and whisk continuously, scraping the base of the pan well. Gradually increase the heat – the sauce needs to emulsify steadily. After 6–8 minutes the mixture will be foamy and creamy, and the temperature should not be higher than 65°C.

Remove from the heat and whisk in the warm clarified butter, then shower in the 30g Parmesan and add the lemon juice and ginger. Season with salt and pepper to taste, then strain through a fine chinois, or leave as it is if you don't mind the odd bit of crushed pepper. Cover with cling film and set aside in a warm place. The sauce must be used within 5–10 minutes of being made.

Pat the halibut steaks dry, season lightly with salt and brush with oil. Brush the ridges of the griddle pan with oil as well, taking care not to burn the brush hairs (you can also use kitchen paper for this).

Place the halibut steaks on the very hot griddle and cook, without moving, for 1½–2 minutes, depending on thickness, then turn them over and cook on the other side for the same time.

To serve, place a halibut steak on each of 4 warmed plates. Sprinkle with the remaining Parmesan, add pepper to taste, then coat half the surface of each piece of fish with the hollandaise sauce. Add a lemon quarter to each plate and serve at once, with any remaining hollandaise served separately in a jug.

Cod steaks with blue cheese butter

60ml grapeseed oil

4 thick, skinless thick cod steaks
(about 160g each)

50ml light olive oil

Sea salt and freshly ground
pepper

For the blue cheese butter

100g butter, softened

120g Stilton, Roquefort or other
well-flavoured blue cheese, most
(or all) of the rind removed

Juice of ½ lemon

4 thyme sprigs, leaves stripped

To serve

16 small semi-confit cherry
tomatoes (see page 248), warmed

1 lemon, quartered

Cod is a firm-fleshed fish that can pair well with a fairly strong cheese, especially when the cheese takes on a golden crust through cooking. I like to serve this dish with quenelles of aubergine purée 'caviar' (see page 116), or simple boiled potatoes coated in parsley butter.

First prepare the flavoured butter. Put the butter into a bowl, add the Stilton or Roquefort and mash into the butter using a fork. Add the lemon juice and thyme leaves and mix until well combined. Season with pepper to taste.

Spoon the flavoured butter onto a large piece of cling film or greaseproof paper and shape into a fat sausage, about 3–4cm in diameter. Wrap in the cling film or paper and twist the ends to secure. Set aside in the fridge.

Heat the grapeseed oil in a frying pan over a medium heat. As soon as it is hot, dab the cod steaks dry and season them very lightly with salt. Add to the pan and cook for 1½–2 minutes then turn them over and cook on the other side for the same time, until nicely golden. They should be not quite cooked in the middle as they will continue to cook out of the pan. Transfer the cod steaks to a wire rack and brush with the olive oil.

Place a cod steak on each of 4 warmed serving plates, then arrange 3 semi-confit cherry tomatoes around each. Add a lemon quarter to each plate and top each cod steak with a couple of thickly sliced rounds of the flavoured butter. Serve at once.

Bleu des Basques

Domaine de Velay

Blu de Bufala

Stilton

Roquefort

Bleu des Causses

Meat, Poultry & Game

Gorgonzola

Chicken cordon bleu

Serves 4

4 skinless chicken supremes (about 150g each)

4 small, thin slices of lightly smoked ham, fat and rind removed

4 small, thin slices of Gruyère (ideally aged for 18–24 months)

2 medium eggs

100g plain flour

150g dried breadcrumbs (ideally panko)

2 thyme sprigs, leaves stripped

150ml grapeseed or groundnut oil

150g butter

Sea salt and freshly ground pepper

1 lemon, quartered, to serve

I adore this staunch classic, which is highly popular and so easy to prepare. You must, of course, serve the chicken supremes as soon as they are cooked, while the Gruyère inside is half-melted and still hot. I like to serve them with spinach – fill a frying pan with washed spinach leaves, add a knob of butter and cook for just 2 minutes.

Using a very sharp knife, cut horizontally three-quarters of the way through each chicken breast at its thickest part, to create a pocket. Slide a slice of ham into each pocket, then place a slice of cheese on top of the ham. Close the pockets and reshape each breast as neatly as possible. Trim away any protruding ham or cheese.

In a shallow bowl, beat the eggs with some salt and pepper. Put the flour into a separate shallow bowl. Mix the breadcrumbs and thyme leaves together in a third, shallow bowl.

Just before cooking (and not before), dip the chicken supremes, one at a time, into the flour to coat lightly, then in the beaten egg and finally in the breadcrumbs to coat all over, patting them so that the crumbs adhere well.

Divide the oil evenly between two frying pans and place over a high heat. Add 40g butter to each, then reduce the heat to medium and place 2 chicken supremes in each pan. Cook for 7 minutes, then turn them over and add the remaining butter to the frying pans, dividing it evenly. Cook for 5–6 minutes, basting the supremes every minute or so, to ensure they cook through evenly.

Transfer the cooked supremes to a wire rack lined with kitchen paper to drain for a minute or two.

Place a chicken supreme on each plate, add a lemon quarter to each and serve with some salad leaves, if you wish.

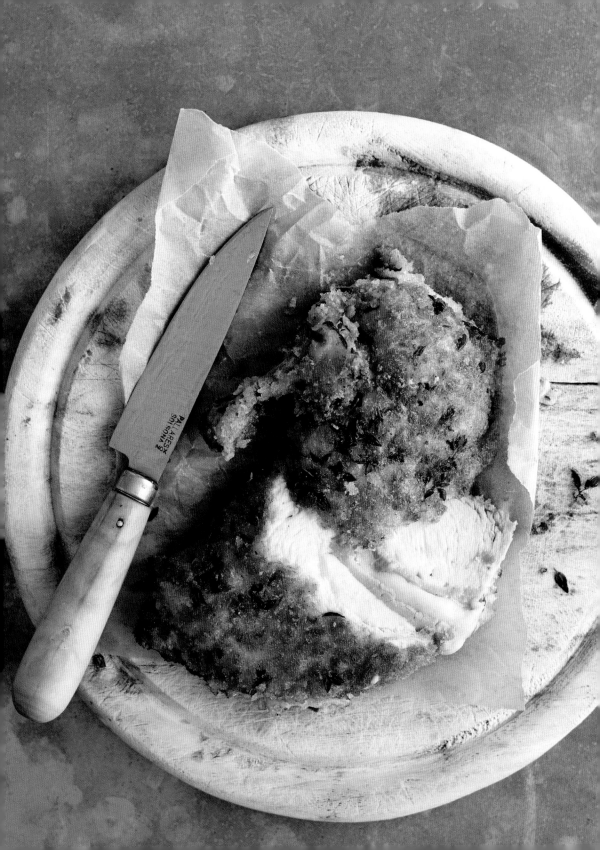

Roast pheasant with Savoy cabbage, bacon and Gorgonzola polenta

SERVES 4

½ Savoy cabbage (about 300g)

120ml grapeseed oil

80g butter

100g Tomme Vaudoise or similar cheese

8 finely sliced rashers of streaky bacon

2 pheasants, preferably hens

50ml water

A bunch of watercress (about 100g), washed and patted dry

Sea salt and freshly ground pepper

For the polenta

300g water

75g polenta (medium-grain)

100g Gorgonzola

2 tbsp grapeseed oil

Pheasant hens are more tender and delicately flavoured than the cocks, so opt for these if you can. The polenta and cabbage – both flavoured with cheese – transform these birds into a delightful game dish. Tomme Vaudoise is a melting soft alpine cheese from Switzerland; if unobtainable you could use another soft cheese instead, such as Morbier or Vacherin Mont d'Or. This is a succulent dish so you won't need to make a sauce or gravy to accompany it.

First make the polenta. Bring the water to the boil in a medium saucepan and, as soon as it boils, shower in the polenta, stirring all the time with a small balloon whisk. Cook over a gentle heat, stirring every 2 or 3 minutes, for 20 minutes, making sure that it doesn't stick to the base of the pan. Remove from the heat and add the Gorgonzola in small pieces, a few at a time, still mixing with a whisk.

Use the 2 tbsp oil to grease the base of a small, shallow rectangular dish, then pour the polenta into the dish and spread evenly into the corners; it should be about 1.5cm deep. Cover with cling film and set aside to cool, then transfer to the fridge.

Cut the cabbage into 2 or 3 pieces. Cut out the thickest part of the core and wash the cabbage in cold water. Drain well, dry and shred finely, using a large chef's knife. Blanch in a pan of boiling water for 2 minutes, then refresh, drain and press lightly between your hands to remove any water.

Heat 50ml of the oil and half the butter in a frying pan over a medium heat. Add the shredded cabbage and sweat for 5 minutes, then increase the heat and cook for another 2–3 minutes. Season lightly with salt and pepper, then remove from the heat and stir in the cheese, in little pieces. Cover the pan with cling film and pierce it in several places with the tip of a knife. Set aside; keep warm.

Preheat the oven to 200°C/Gas 6.

continued overleaf

continued from previous page

Wrap 4 bacon slices around each pheasant to cover the breast, overlapping them very slightly. Secure with kitchen string, tied around the birds a few times and/or use cocktail sticks through the bacon and into the fleshy parts of the thighs, to make sure the bacon stays in place as it cooks.

Using your fingertips, use 50ml of the remaining oil to coat the entire surface of both pheasants. Place in a roasting dish and roast in the oven for 15 minutes. Take the dish from the oven, turn the pheasants over and pour the water into the dish. Roast for a further 10 minutes.

When the pheasants are cooked, take them out of the oven and baste with the reduced liquor in the dish. Place the pheasants, breast down, in a warm dish, and baste again. Loosely cover with foil and set aside to rest for 5–10 minutes.

Heat the remaining 20ml oil and 40g butter in a frying pan over a medium heat. Cut 4 neat triangles from the chilled set polenta and add to the pan. Fry for 2 minutes on each side until golden, then remove and drain on kitchen paper.

To serve, remove the string and/or cocktail sticks holding the bacon in place on the pheasants, then remove a breast with a leg attached from each, to give 4 portions.

Place the pheasant portions on warmed plates and arrange a polenta triangle on each, along with a little bacon and a few watercress leaves. Sprinkle with a little salt and serve at once, with the cabbage offered separately in a large bowl, or divided between the plates.

Steak tartare

SERVES 4

500g very chilled, almost freezing cold, beef fillet

1 egg yolk, plus 4 extra yolks to serve

2 tsp Dijon mustard

2 tsp Worcestershire sauce

6 drops of Tabasco

1 tsp grated horseradish, ideally fresh, or from a jar

2 anchovy fillets in oil, finely chopped

1½ tbsp light fruity olive oil

5g curly-leaf parsley, chopped

1 small tsp baby capers, drained and chopped

4 small gherkins, finely diced

2 tsp finely chopped onion

50g Parmigiano Reggiano, finely grated

Sea salt and freshly ground pepper

1–2 lemons, cut into wedges, to finish and serve

For the Melba toast

2 slices of medium-cut white sandwich loaf

The pleasure of this dish is sharing it between friends, as the ritual of mixing and seasoning creates a special moment of conviviality. The Parmesan adds a very pleasing note, and homemade French fries or the skinnier *pommes allumettes* are undoubtedly the companion *par excellence* to this dish. Everyone is fond of Melba toast, and so I often make extra to serve on the side. (Illustrated on previous page.)

Trim the fillet of beef and cut into fine dice (*brunoise*). Place in a bowl, cover with cling film and return to the fridge to keep it chilled while you assemble the rest of the ingredients in saucers or small bowls, ready to mix at the table, and prepare the Melba toast.

For the Melba toast, preheat the grill. Using a knife, trim the crusts from the bread slices. Grill the bread on both sides, then split each slice horizontally in two with a knife to make 4 thin slices. Toast the uncooked bready sides to make 4 thin Melba toast slices.

To serve, put the beef into a large bowl set over another bowl of ice at the table. Place all the other steak tartare ingredients on the table, with spoons. Gradually add these ingredients to the meat in the order listed, keeping back the 4 extra yolks, mixing with a large wooden spoon. (You may prefer to omit some of the ingredients, according to preference.) Taste the mixture from time to time as you are mixing, to make sure the seasoning is right, and invite your guests to do the same – this is part of the ritual and gives everyone a chance to offer their opinion. Squeeze over some of the lemon at the end.

Once you are satisfied with the result, place a piece of Melba toast on each of 4 chilled plates. Place a plain cutter, about 8cm in diameter, on another chilled plate and fill it with the meat mixture, pressing it in lightly with the back of a spoon, then use the back of the spoon to make a small dip in the centre.

Slide a large palette knife under the steak tartare and carefully lift it onto one of the Melba toasts. Remove the pastry cutter by lifting and turning it gently. Repeat with the remaining mixture to make another 3 steak tartares. Place an egg yolk in the small dip in the middle of each one. Serve a couple of lemon wedges on the side of each plate.

Gratinated veal chops

SERVES 4

50ml light olive oil

1 medium aubergine or
2 courgettes, trimmed and
cut into cubes

1 garlic clove, finely chopped

200g piece of Emmenthal

4 veal chops (about 220g each)

3 tbsp grainy mustard (ideally
Meaux)

1 egg yolk

80g butter

100ml dry white wine

20g tarragon sprigs, leaves
stripped and finely snipped

Sea salt and freshly ground
pepper

The flavours of veal and Emmenthal marry perfectly in this easy-to-prepare dish and tarragon adds a lovely fragrance to the accompanying jus.

Heat the olive oil in a frying pan over a medium heat, then add the aubergine or courgette cubes. Cook, stirring every few minutes, for 8 minutes if using courgettes or 15 minutes for aubergine. Add the garlic, season lightly with salt and grind in some pepper. Cook for another minute then take off the heat; keep warm.

Cut 4 fine slices from the piece of Emmenthal, then trim each slice into a circle, just smaller than the surface of the veal chops.

Using a very sharp knife, cut horizontally through each chop until you reach the bone, to create a sort of pocket, making sure that the opening isn't too big. Slide a circle of Emmenthal into each veal pocket, keeping it flat and making sure the cheese is all contained within the pocket.

Grate the remaining cheese on a medium grating disc and put into a bowl with the mustard and egg yolk. Mix with a spoon to combine.

Heat 50g of the butter in a large frying pan over a medium heat. When it is hot, add the veal chops, season lightly with salt and cook for 2–3 minutes on each side for rare, or 3 minutes on each side for medium-rare (*à point*). Remove from the pan to a wire rack set over a plate; keep warm.

Pour off the excess butter from the frying pan, then pour in the wine, stirring and scraping to deglaze. Let bubble over a medium heat to reduce by half. Add the tarragon, then take off the heat and incorporate the remaining 30g butter, a small piece at a time, stirring with a small balloon whisk. Transfer this jus to a small saucepan and keep warm.

Preheat the grill to high. Place the veal chops on the grill rack and spoon the cheese mixture on top to cover the surface of the meat completely. Grill for 1–2 minutes until golden and bubbling. Place a chop on each warmed plate and spoon the aubergine or courgette to one side. Pour the jus around the other side and serve.

Meatballs with Gouda

750g lean beef, minced on
a medium setting

250g lean pork, minced on
a medium setting

1 garlic clove, finely chopped

A pinch of ground cloves

A pinch of ground cinnamon

Finely grated zest and juice of
1 lemon

A pinch of dried oregano

20g Parmesan, freshly grated

1 medium egg, plus 1 extra yolk

50ml cold milk

140g Gouda, cut into 18 cubes

60g dried fine breadcrumbs

100ml grapeseed oil

Sea salt and freshly ground pepper

For the tomato coulis

50ml light olive oil

1 garlic clove, finely chopped

1 thyme sprig, leaves stripped and
finely chopped

300g tomatoes, peeled, deseeded
and chopped

5g basil leaves, finely snipped

To serve

1 medium aubergine, trimmed

50ml light olive oil

Flat-leaf parsley, to garnish

This is a good family-style dish. The melting cheese in the meatballs blends harmoniously with the surrounding meat. You could use Raclette or another semi-firm cheese in place of the Gouda. Sautéed aubergine is the perfect complement; for a more substantial dish, I serve seasoned macaroni too.

To make the tomato coulis, heat the olive oil in a saucepan over a medium heat. Add the garlic and thyme and cook, stirring, for 30 seconds, then add the tomatoes. Bring to a simmer and cook gently for 5 minutes, then add the basil and salt and pepper to taste. Transfer to a blender and blitz for 45 seconds, then strain through a chinois into the rinsed-out pan; keep warm.

Preheat the oven to 200°C/Gas 6.

For the meatballs, put the minced meats, garlic, ground spices, lemon zest and juice, oregano, Parmesan, 1 tsp salt and a generous grinding of pepper into a large bowl. Beat the egg and extra yolk together and add to the bowl. Mix well. Add the milk and mix again.

Take about 50g of the meat mixture and place it in the cupped palm of one hand. Push a cube of cheese into the middle, then shape into a ball enclosing the cheese in the meat using both palms. Repeat to make 18 meatballs in total, using the remaining meat and cheese.

Spread out the breadcrumbs on a small tray or large plate. Place 6 meatballs at a time in the breadcrumbs and roll them to coat evenly, then transfer to a plate or board.

Heat the grapeseed oil in a large frying pan over a high heat, add the meatballs and fry for 2–3 minutes until lightly golden all over. Transfer to a roasting dish and cook in the oven for 6–8 minutes.

Meanwhile, cut the aubergine into thick batons. Heat the olive oil in a sauté pan, add the batons and cook over a medium heat, stirring occasionally, for 6–8 minutes. Season with salt and pepper to taste.

To serve, divide the tomato coulis between 6 warmed plates and place 3 meatballs on top. Add the aubergine batons and garnish with flat-leaf parsley. Serve at once, with buttered macaroni on the side if you wish.

Peppered steaks with blue cheese sauce and potato millefeuilles

SERVES 2

2 sirloin steaks (about 220g each, trimmed weight)

30g black peppercorns, very roughly crushed

2 tbsp grapeseed oil

For the potato millefeuille

1 very large potato, peeled and washed

30g clarified butter, melted

3g chervil sprigs, snipped

30g Parmigiano Reggiano, freshly grated

5g flat-leaf parsley, snipped

Sea salt and freshly ground pepper

For the blue cheese sauce

30g butter

1 shallot (60g), finely chopped

100ml good-quality red wine vinegar

5g tarragon leaves, snipped, plus extra to garnish

100ml chicken stock (see page 244 for home-made)

85ml double cream

60g Bleu des Causses or other crumbly, not too strong, blue cheese

Peppered sirloin steaks are taken to a new level with a lively blue cheese sauce. The potato millefeuille can be made ahead and reheated under the grill. (Illustrated on previous page.)

For the potato millefeuille, thinly slice the potato lengthways into 2mm slices. Lay a double layer of cling film, about 40cm square, on your work surface. Dip a slice of potato in the clarified butter, place in the middle of the cling film and sprinkle with a little chervil and Parmesan. Dip a second potato slice in the butter and place on the first slice. Sprinkle with parsley and Parmesan. Continue layering in this way, adding a little salt and plenty of pepper to the layers, until all the potato slices are used and you have a stack. Bring the cling film up over the potato and wrap well to seal.

Place the millefeuille in a steamer and steam gently for 1½ hours, topping up the water as necessary. Lift out onto a plate. Let cool slightly, still wrapped, then lay a small board on the potato and put a 250–500g weight on top, to press the potato without crushing it. Once cooled, refrigerate, with the weight in position, for 2–3 hours.

For the sauce, melt the butter in a small pan over a low heat. Add the shallot and sweat for 1 minute, then pour in the wine vinegar and let bubble to reduce by half. Add the tarragon and stock and simmer for 20 minutes. Add the cream and reduce until thickened enough to coat the back of a spoon. Season and keep warm. Preheat the grill.

To prepare the steaks, coat both sides with the crushed black pepper, pressing with the palm of your hand so that it sticks. Heat the oil in a frying pan over a medium heat. When hot, add the steaks and cook over a high heat for 1 minute on each side for rare, 1½ minutes on each side for medium-rare (*à point*), or 3 minutes on each side for well done. Transfer the steaks to a wire rack to rest for 1 minute.

Unwrap the potato millefeuille and cut lengthways into 1cm thick slices. Place under the hot grill for 1–2 minutes. Place the steaks and sliced potato on warmed plates. Roughly crumble the blue cheese into the sauce, then spoon over half of each steak. Garnish with tarragon and serve at once, with the remaining sauce on the side.

Pan-fried calf's liver with a Parmesan and sesame seed coating

SERVES 4

2½ tbsp grapeseed or other vegetable oil

60g Parmigiano Reggiano, plus 15g to serve

50g toasted white sesame seeds

4 thin slices of calf's liver (about 120g each)

40g butter, melted and cooled until barely tepid

Sea salt

1 lemon, quartered, to serve

This finely balanced, flavourful dish is particularly good served with dauphine potatoes (see page 192) and, or, salad leaves dressed with a lemon vinaigrette.

Heat the oil in a large non-stick frying pan over a medium heat.

Meanwhile, finely grate the Parmesan and, using a fork, gently mix it with the toasted sesame seeds and a pinch of salt on a plate.

Brush the liver slices very lightly with the cooled melted butter, then place them, one at a time, in the sesame and Parmesan mixture and press down well with your fingertips so that the coating adheres to the liver.

Increase the heat under the frying pan and add the coated liver slices, taking care as the oil may splutter and the sesame seeds will pop as they cook. Cook for 1 minute, then turn the slices over and cook on the other side for another minute, for pink liver.

Remove from the heat and immediately place a slice of liver on each warmed serving plate. Grate a little Parmesan on top of each liver slice, add a lemon quarter to each plate and serve straight away.

Moussaka

SERVES 6

4 aubergines (about 300g each)

About 200ml light olive oil

2 large potatoes (about 400g in total), peeled and cut lengthways into 3mm slices

1 garlic clove, crushed

1 thyme sprig

1 bay leaf

1 litre béchamel sauce (see page 246, double quantity)

A pinch of freshly grated nutmeg

1 egg yolk

125g Kefalotyri cheese, grated

Sea salt and freshly ground pepper

For the filling

50ml light olive oil

400g lean beef, minced on a medium setting

1 onion (125g), finely chopped

1 garlic clove, finely chopped

1 carrot (about 60g), finely diced

50g celery, finely diced

75g tomato purée

A pinch of ground cinnamon

A pinch of ground cloves

300ml water

To garnish (optional)

20g flat-leaf parsley, deep-fried

All the components for this dish can be prepared in advance, ready to assemble an hour or so before serving. Kefalotyri gives the dish its authenticity but you can use Cheddar or Gruyère instead. I like to serve a salad of finely sliced fennel, cucumber, cherry tomatoes, red onion and lemon on the side.

To prepare the filling, heat the olive oil in a large sauté pan over a high heat. Add the beef and cook, stirring often, for 2 minutes to brown lightly. Add the remaining ingredients one at a time. Once the water is added, reduce the heat to low and cook until the liquid has reduced almost totally. Tip into a bowl, cover and set aside.

Preheat the oven to 220°C/Gas 7. Halve 3 aubergines lengthways, then cut a 5mm criss-cross pattern in the flesh. Brush the scored flesh with 50ml olive oil and season with salt and pepper. Wrap each aubergine half in foil and bake for 25–30 minutes. Unwrap and, when cool enough to handle, scoop out the flesh with a spoon, leaving a 3mm thick layer next to the skin. Set the aubergine shells aside.

Roughly chop the scooped-out flesh and put into a large bowl. Mix in 20ml olive oil, then check the seasoning. Cover and set aside.

Heat a ridged griddle pan. Cut the fourth aubergine lengthways into 6 slices. Oil generously, salt lightly and griddle for 30 seconds, then give them a quarter-turn and cook for another 30 seconds. Turn carefully and repeat on the other side. Set aside on a plate.

Heat 75ml olive oil in a frying pan over a medium heat. Add the potatoes with the garlic, thyme and bay leaf and cook until lightly golden and tender. Season, drain and set aside in a bowl.

Reheat the béchamel in a pan over a low heat to a simmer, then remove from the heat, add the nutmeg and whisk in the egg yolk. Mix in two-thirds of the grated cheese.

Put the reserved aubergine shells in an oiled roasting tin and divide the potato slices between them. Add a layer of chopped aubergine, a slice of griddled aubergine and finally the meat filling, piling it up generously. Spoon on the sauce to coat generously and sprinkle with the remaining cheese. Bake for 20–25 minutes until bubbling and golden on top. Serve garnished with deep-fried parsley, if you like.

Baked stuffed tomatoes with lamb and summer vegetables

SERVES 6

6 beef tomatoes (350–400g each)

1 small aubergine (about 200g)

Juice of 1 lemon

1 red pepper (about 150g), cored, deseeded and cut into strips

1 small courgette (about 160g), peeled and cut into small pieces

170ml olive oil

1 large onion (about 150g), finely chopped

1 small fennel bulb (about 120g), finely chopped

2 garlic cloves, finely chopped

150g long-grain rice

75g flat-leaf parsley leaves

30g mint leaves

200g lamb shoulder, minced on a medium setting

30g fresh white breadcrumbs (ideally one-day old)

240g Mastelo, mozzarella or goat's cheese log, cut into 12 slices

Sea salt and freshly ground pepper

As you bake this dish, wonderful aromas will suffuse your kitchen and table. The stuffed tomatoes are also excellent reheated the next day, if you happen to have one or two left over. (Illustrated on previous page.)

Slice off the top quarter of each tomato and set aside. Using a small knife and a spoon, scoop out the inside of each tomato; reserve the flesh but discard the seeds. Set the tomato 'shells' aside.

Peel the aubergine, cut into small pieces and toss with the lemon juice. Place in a food processor with the red pepper, courgette and reserved tomato flesh. Blitz for 3–4 minutes to make a coulis.

Heat 120ml of the olive oil in a heavy-based pan over a medium heat. Add the onion and sweat for 2 minutes, then add the fennel and cook for a further 2 minutes. Add the garlic followed by the coulis. Bring to the boil, then stir in the rice. Remove from the heat and leave to cool completely.

Preheat the oven to 220°C/Gas 7. Use the remaining olive oil to oil the base of a shallow roasting dish.

Finely chop the parsley and mint together. Add the minced lamb to the cold vegetable and rice mixture. Stir to combine, then mix in the chopped herbs and breadcrumbs. Season well with salt and pepper.

Season the tomato cavities and one-third fill with the stuffing mix. Place a slice of cheese on the stuffing, then fill the tomatoes almost to the brim with more stuffing. Top with another slice of cheese and press it lightly down into the stuffing. Replace the tomato 'lids'.

Place the stuffed tomatoes in the prepared dish and pour about 100ml hot water around them. Bake for 30 minutes. Baste the tomatoes with the cooking juices, lower the oven setting to 200°C/ Gas 6 and return to the oven for a further 45 minutes.

Transfer the stuffed tomatoes to warmed plates and spoon over a little of the cooking juices to serve.

Braised oxtail with Pecorino

SERVES 4

100ml grapeseed oil

1.4kg large oxtails, trimmed of excess fat, soaked in cold water for 1 hour, drained, cut into pieces at the joints and patted dry

2 onions, roughly chopped

4 garlic cloves, crushed

400g carrots, thickly sliced

75cl bottle of red wine (ideally Pinot noir)

400ml ready-made veal stock, or home-made rich chicken stock (see page 244)

1 bouquet garni (thyme sprig, bay leaf and a few parsley stalks, tied together)

½ celeriac, peeled, cut into cubes and blanched for a few minutes

300g button mushrooms, cut into large pieces

20g curly-leaf parsley, chopped

150g Pecorino Romano, finely grated

Sea salt and freshly ground pepper

Pecorino is often served with roast or grilled lamb but I also adore it with oxtail. This is an exceptionally delicious dish, with the grated cheese partially sticking to the meltingly soft meat. Use your fingers to pick up the bones and suck out the lovely marrow and juices. You could use another hard cheese aged between 6 and 12 months in place of the Pecorino.

Preheat the oven to 170°C/Gas 3½.

Heat the oil in a large sauté or frying pan over a medium heat and brown the oxtail pieces, turning them to colour well on each side. Remove with a slotted spoon and set aside in a colander.

Add the onions, garlic and carrots to the oil remaining in the pan and cook, stirring constantly, for 2–3 minutes until lightly golden. Drain and set aside with the oxtail.

Bring the wine to the boil in a large flameproof casserole over a high heat and let bubble for 5 minutes. Pour in the stock then add the oxtail pieces, onion and carrot mixture and the bouquet garni. As it comes to a simmer, put the lid on and transfer to the oven.

Cook for 2 hours, then add the celeriac and mushrooms and return to the oven, covered, to cook for a further 30 minutes until the meat is meltingly tender.

Remove from the oven and use a skimmer to transfer the oxtail pieces and vegetables to a shallow serving dish. Cover with cling film and keep warm.

Strain the cooking liquor through a fine chinois into a saucepan, discarding the bouquet garni. Skim off the fat from the surface, then place the pan over a medium heat and allow the liquor to bubble and reduce to a full-flavoured, concentrated jus that will lightly coat the back of a spoon.

To serve, pour about one-third of the reduced jus over the oxtail and vegetables and sprinkle with the chopped parsley and then the grated cheese. Serve the remaining jus separately in a jug.

Confit of pork belly with pappardelle and cheese

SERVES 6

800g–1kg piece of pork belly, well layered with fat

1 orange

1 lemon

4 thyme sprigs

100ml oil from the semi-confit cherry tomatoes (see below)

400ml cold water

200ml light olive oil

150g tomato purée

1 garlic clove, chopped

150g Greek flower cheese or ricotta

150g Mizithra (Greek fresh sheep or goat's cheese)

½ onion (about 75g), peeled and finely chopped

4 tbsp red wine vinegar

30g sultanas, blanched for 1 minute and drained

½ apple, preferably Granny Smith, cut into fine julienne

10 sage leaves, snipped

400g dried pappardelle

10 semi-confit cherry tomatoes (see page 248)

Freshly ground pepper

I had the pleasure of sampling this rustic, flavourful dish in Greece. If you cannot obtain Mizithra cheese, use Kefalotyri or Pecorino Romano instead. The pork belly, should you have any left over, is delicious cut into thick lardons and pan-fried, then added to a salad of frisée or dandelion leaves, with a little strong cheese crumbled over. You need to start preparing this dish at least 24 hours in advance.

Preheat the oven to 220°C/Gas 7.

Rinse the pork belly in cold water. Pat dry then, using a very sharp knife, make incisions, 2mm deep, in several places through the rind, to assist the cooking.

Finely pare the zest from the orange and lemon and set aside. Slice the orange and lemon across into rounds, about 2mm thick, then spread the slices out in a shallow roasting dish and scatter over the thyme sprigs.

Lightly oil the pork rind, using some of the cooled oil from the semi-confit cherry tomatoes – dipping your fingers into the oil and using them to spread it. Place the pork, rind side up, on top of the citrus slices, then pour the cold water into the dish (not over the meat).

Roast for 30 minutes, then lower the oven setting to 150°C/Gas 2 and baste the pork rind with the cooking juices. Roast for a further 2 hours, basting every 30 minutes with the cooking juices.

Remove the pork from the oven and set aside to cool in the cooking juices. Once cooled, carefully transfer to a baking sheet or large ceramic dish. Cover with cling film then place a tray on top of the pork and weight it down, using a 3–5kg weight, so that the tray presses heavily down on the pork. Refrigerate for at least 24 hours, and up to 48 hours.

continued overleaf

continued from previous page

Strain the pork cooking juices into a pan through a fine chinois and let bubble to reduce until thick enough to lightly coat the back of a spoon; set aside for the sauce.

For the tomato sauce, put the 200ml olive oil, tomato purée, garlic, flower or ricotta cheese and 100g of the Mizithra cheese in a food processor or blender and blitz for 1–2 minutes until smooth. Transfer to a bowl and set aside.

Heat the remaining tomato confit oil in a large frying pan. Add the onion, then after 1 minute add the wine vinegar. Let bubble to reduce by half then add the reduced pork juices, tomato sauce and sultanas and simmer over a gentle heat for 15 minutes. Finally, add the apple and sage.

Meanwhile, bring a large pan of water to the boil and salt well. Add the pappardelle and cook for 7–9 minutes until *al dente* (cooked but firm to the bite).

While the pasta is cooking, heat the confit cherry tomatoes through over a gentle heat for a few minutes.

Drain the pappardelle as soon as it is ready, then tip it into the sauce in the pan and mix lightly. Add the semi-confit tomatoes and fork through gently.

Using a knife, remove a section of the pork rind then, using a fork, shred the pork flesh by scraping it out with the ends of the fork. Add the shredded pork to the pasta and sauce and mix through gently with the fork. Season with pepper to taste; there should be no need to add salt.

To serve, crumble over the remaining 50g Mizithra cheese, and sprinkle with the reserved orange and lemon zest. Serve at once, straight from the pan, so everyone can help themselves.

Chicory and ham gratin

SERVES 4

8 chicory bulbs (about 80g each)

1 lemon, quartered

80g butter

160g Gruyère, Comté or Cheddar, grated

1 litre béchamel sauce (see page 246, double quantity)

2 pinches of finely grated nutmeg

40g crème fraîche

8 small, fine slices of cured ham on the bone, or very good quality cooked ham

Sea salt and freshly ground pepper

Inexpensive and easy to put together, this tempting gratin can be embellished with all manner of cheeses. It can be prepared a day ahead and kept in the fridge; just allow an extra 10 minutes in the oven.

Bring a large pan of water to the boil and salt lightly. Remove the outermost leaves from the chicory bulbs. Using a small knife, make 2 incisions into the stalk end of each, which will help this thicker part of the chicory cook.

Lower the chicory bulbs into the boiling water and add the lemon quarters and half the butter. Simmer, covered, for 20–30 minutes. To check if the chicory is cooked, insert the tip of a knife into a stalk end; it should slide in easily. Remove from the heat and leave the chicory in the cooking water for about 10 minutes, then drain and refresh in cold water without cooling them completely. Gently transfer the chicory bulbs, one at a time, to a colander.

Preheat the oven to 180°C/Gas 4. Use the remaining butter to grease a shallow ovenproof gratin dish that will hold the chicory in a single layer and sprinkle a little of the grated cheese evenly over the base.

Heat up the béchamel in a saucepan over a low heat and add the nutmeg. As soon as it comes to a simmer, stir in the crème fraîche and season with salt and pepper to taste. Set aside; keep warm.

Gently squeeze each chicory bulb – just enough to remove any excess water. Roll a slice of ham around each one and arrange side by side in the gratin dish. Cover with the béchamel then sprinkle the remaining cheese generously over the top.

Cook in the oven for 20–25 minutes until nicely golden on top. Place the dish on the table and let everyone serve themselves, taking care with the first mouthful, as it will be very hot.

Pasta, Rice & Bread

Pecorino Romano

Spaghetti with Pecorino and black pepper

SERVES 4

320g medium spaghetti

200g Pecorino Romano, freshly grated

10g freshly, coarsely grated black pepper, plus extra to serve

Salt

You will come across this incredibly simple dish – *cacio e pepe* – on restaurant menus all over Rome. Its success lies in the Pecorino being of the highest quality, cooking the pasta to perfection, and getting the consistency of the sauce (which is something like a *beurre blanc*) just right.

Bring a large pan of lightly salted water to the boil, add the spaghetti and cook, stirring from time to time, until *al dente* (tender but firm to the bite). Drain immediately, reserving about a cupful of the cooking water, and return the spaghetti to the pan, adding about 50ml of the reserved water.

Shower in the grated Pecorino, stirring with a wooden spoon as you do so, to create a creamy sauce, adding a little more cooking water if necessary. Add the pepper and toss briefly to mix.

Swirl a quarter of the spaghetti around a fork, then arrange in a tall mound in the middle of a warmed deep plate. Repeat with the remaining spaghetti for the other 3 warmed bowls, then drizzle the sauce left in the pan over each mound. Sprinkle with a little more pepper and serve at once.

Prosciutto and cheese ravioli with grilled ceps

Serves 6

For the pasta

250g '00' Italian flour

1 medium egg

4 egg yolks

2 tsp cold water

2 tsp light olive oil

A pinch of salt

For the filling and broth

2 attractive, nicely firm ceps (about 300g in total)

50ml light, fruity olive oil

300g cottage cheese

120g Parmigiano Reggiano, freshly grated

25g baby capers, rinsed and dried

30g fines herbes (equal quantities of fresh flat-leaf parsley, chives and chervil), snipped, plus 6 chervil sprigs, to garnish

100g prosciutto, cut into fine strips then into dice

1.5 litres chicken stock (see page 244 for homemade, or use shop-bought)

1 small courgette, finely sliced into long julienne

5g fresh ginger, peeled and grated

Sea salt and freshly ground pepper

This exquisite dish takes a while to prepare but don't let that put you off. The pasta can be made 24 hours in advance and kept tightly wrapped in cling film in the fridge. And you can adjust the size of the ravioli if you like, shaping and cutting 12 smaller ravioli from the rolled-out pasta. The ginger that is added at the last minute lends a lovely freshness to the chicken broth.

To make the pasta, pile the flour into a mound on your work surface and make a well in the centre. Add the egg and egg yolks to the well, with the cold water, oil and salt. Using your fingertips, mix together the ingredients in the well, then gradually work in the flour. When the ingredients are almost combined, work the mixture with the palm of your hand 4 or 5 times, then gather it into a ball, wrap in cling film and leave to rest in the fridge for at least 1 hour.

Wipe the ceps using a slightly dampened tea towel to remove any impurities or traces of sand or grit. Detach the stalks and cut them into fine dice, then slice the caps lengthways into 3mm thick slices. Set aside the 12 nicest looking, larger slices on a plate and oil them lightly with olive oil. Finely dice the rest of the cep slices and add them to the diced stalks.

Heat a few drops of olive oil in a frying pan, then add the diced ceps and cook over a medium heat for 1½ minutes. Sprinkle lightly with salt and set aside in a bowl. Heat a ridged griddle pan over a high heat, add the cep slices and cook for 30 seconds, then turn and griddle on the other side for 30 seconds. Set aside on a plate.

To make the filling, in a bowl, mix together the cottage cheese, Parmesan, capers, fines herbes, diced prosciutto and cooled diced ceps. Season lightly with salt and a generous grinding of pepper. Cover with cling film and set aside.

continued overleaf

continued from previous page

Divide the pasta dough in half; re-wrap one half. Roll out the other half using a pasta machine, starting with the rollers set to 2cm then progressively narrowing the setting until the pasta is rolled out to a sheet 1.5mm thick. It should be 12–13cm wide and 36–40cm long. Cover with a tea towel to prevent it from drying out. Roll out the other half in the same way, to the same thickness and dimensions. Cover with a tea towel as well, to prevent it from drying out.

Using a spoon, divide the filling mixture into 6 mounds. Uncover one sheet of dough and place the mounds along the middle, spacing them at regular intervals. Brush a little cold water around each filling mound. Now uncover the second sheet of pasta dough and position it over the top of the filling, without stretching it (or only very lightly), so that it is covering the whole of the lower sheet of dough and the mounds of filling.

Using your fingertips, press the top sheet of pasta gently all around each mound of filling, to seal the 2 sheets of pasta together well, and so avoid any filling escaping during cooking. Using a fluted 10cm pastry cutter, cut out each ravioli individually, then place on a very clean, flat surface. Brush off any excess flour from them.

Heat the chicken stock in a large pan over a medium heat.

Gently lower the ravioli into the boiling chicken stock and cook over a gentle heat for 2–3 minutes for *al dente*, or 4–5 minutes for a softer result. Carefully remove the ravioli from the stock using a slotted spoon or skimmer and place on a very clean tea towel. Increase the heat under the stock pan and add the courgette julienne. Cook for 30 seconds, then remove with a skimmer.

Place each ravioli in a warmed shallow bowl and surround with the courgette and grilled ceps. Add the ginger to the stock, stir and check the seasoning. Spoon some stock into each bowl (as much or as little as you prefer). Garnish with chervil and serve at once.

Macaroni and mushroom gratin

200g button mushrooms

80g butter

1 small shallot, finely chopped

Juice of ½ lemon

400g macaroni (short 'elbow' type)

500ml béchamel sauce (see page 246)

80g crème fraîche

140g Comté, Emmenthal, Gruyère, Cheddar or other hard cheese, grated

Sea salt and freshly ground pepper

Almost any hard cheese in the world would be good in this gratin, as long as it's young (aged 3–4 months), meaning it will be rich and smooth but not too strong in flavour. It is lovely served with a lightly dressed salad for lunch, or as an accompaniment to roast veal, pork or poultry.

Carefully peel the mushrooms using a small knife, and wipe clean using slightly moistened kitchen paper. Cut into 2–3mm thick slices.

Melt 60g of the butter in a frying pan over a medium heat. Add the shallot, followed by the sliced mushrooms. Sprinkle with a little salt and cook for 2–3 minutes. Add the lemon juice and stir every minute or so, until the liquid released by the mushrooms has evaporated. Tip into a small bowl and set aside.

Preheat the oven to 180°C/Gas 4.

Bring a large pan of lightly salted water to the boil, then add the macaroni, stir once with a wooden spoon and cook until *al dente*, about 5–7 minutes.

Meanwhile, heat the béchamel in a saucepan over a low heat until it is simmering, then stir in the crème fraîche and season with salt and pepper to taste.

As soon as the macaroni is cooked, drain it and tip into a large bowl. Pour over the béchamel and mix with a wooden spoon, then fold through the mushrooms and about two-thirds of the grated cheese until evenly combined. Taste and adjust the seasoning.

Use the remaining butter to grease a gratin dish, then sprinkle a little of the remaining cheese over the base and sides. Tip the macaroni mixture into the dish and spread it out evenly, without packing it down, then scatter the rest of the cheese over the surface. Cook in the oven for 15–20 minutes until bubbling and nicely golden on top.

Serve straight from the dish, taking care as it will be piping hot.

Cep and Parmesan risotto

SERVES 4

250g ceps (ideally fresh, see note)

80ml light olive oil

1 onion (about 100g), finely chopped

300g Carnaroli or Arborio rice

150ml dry white wine

1–1.2 litres warm vegetable stock (see page 245) or water

10g flat-leaf parsley, finely chopped

120g butter, cut into small pieces

80g Parmigiano Reggiano (ideally aged for 12 months), freshly grated

Sea salt and freshly ground black pepper

The success of a risotto lies in the cooking technique, which calls for your almost continuous attention throughout. The Parmesan can be replaced with Pecorino if you like, though it won't deliver quite the same flavour.

Using a small knife, peel the cep stems then gently wipe the ceps using a damp tea towel or kitchen paper. Chop the stems and slice the caps into slivers.

Heat 60ml of the olive oil in a heavy-based pan over a gentle heat. Add the onion and sweat for 2 minutes, then shower in the rice, stirring with a spatula as you do so. Cook, stirring, for 2 minutes then add the wine, still stirring, and increase the heat to medium.

Once the wine has been absorbed, add the stock or water, a small ladleful at a time, stirring constantly. It is important to add the liquid gradually and to stir frequently, as this will allow the risotto to develop its characteristic creamy consistency.

Meanwhile, heat the remaining 20ml olive oil in a frying pan over a medium heat. Add the chopped cep stems and sauté for 1 minute then add the sliced caps and cook for 3–4 minutes, according to how you prefer them. Sprinkle with a little salt, add the chopped parsley and transfer to a bowl; keep warm.

When the risotto has absorbed enough liquid to achieve the desired consistency, remove from the heat. Holding the handle of the pan and swirling gently, mix in the butter a few pieces at a time, then the Parmesan and finally the hot ceps.

Season the risotto with pepper to taste and divide between warmed plates or bowls. Serve at once.

If fresh ceps are unavailable, replace with 50g dried and soak them in warm water to cover generously for 20–30 minutes. Drain, reserving the soaking liquor and use this as part of the liquid added to the rice. Sauté the soaked ceps and add them to the risotto just 2 minutes before the end of cooking (before adding the butter and Parmesan).

Focaccia with cheese

Serves 6

250g 'type 55' flour or white bread flour, plus extra for dusting

100ml water, at room temperature

35ml light olive oil, plus 4 tsp to oil the tin and to finish

1 tsp fine sea salt

250g Stracchino (also called Crescenza) cheese, cut into small pieces

About ½ tsp flaky sea salt

Focaccia is highly prized in the Ligurian village of Rocco, where it has been awarded AOC (*appellation d'origine contrôlée*) status. It is best eaten as soon as it comes out of the oven, or at least while still hot. Accompanied by a few salad leaves, focaccia makes a delicious starter, or you can cut it into slim slices to serve with an aperitif. (Also illustrated overleaf.)

Put the flour, water, olive oil and fine sea salt into the bowl of a stand mixer fitted with the dough hook and mix on a slow speed for 1 minute. Use a rubber spatula to bring the mixture from the sides towards the hook or paddle, then continue to mix on a medium speed until the dough is homogeneous and very smooth. Cover the bowl with cling film and set aside to rest at room temperature for at least 15 minutes.

If you happen to have a pizza oven, heat it to 300°C. Otherwise preheat the oven to 250°C/Gas 10 or as hot as it will go. Grease a loose-based flan tin, about 26cm in diameter, with 2 tsp olive oil.

Divide the dough in half. Using generously floured fingers, stretch out one half until it is thin enough to see through. Place this piece in the flan tin, gently pressing it into the edges of the tin and allowing the excess to overhanging the rim. Distribute the pieces of cheese evenly over the dough.

Repeat the stretching with the second piece of dough, then position this over the tin. Using your fingertips, lightly press the edges of the dough together all the way around, to seal. Using a small knife, cut away the excess around the edge of the tin – this will be up to 30–40% of the dough. (If you like, you can roll this excess into a rectangle, sprinkle with oil and bake as a separate plain focaccia.)

Using the tip of the small knife, make 6–8 holes in the top to allow the steam to escape during baking. Drizzle the remaining 2 tsp olive oil over the surface and sprinkle with the flaky salt. Bake for about 4–5 minutes if using a pizza oven, or 6–8 minutes if using a standard oven. Serve cut into wedges.

Roquefort pizza with pear, honey and almonds

SERVES 6–8

For the dough

10g fresh yeast

185ml tepid water

325g 'type 55' flour, plus extra for dusting

12g fine sea salt

12ml light olive oil

For the topping

150g Roquefort, ideally not too ripe or soft

60g thin honey

2 pears, not too ripe

A squeeze of lemon juice

1 clove, crushed with the flat of a knife, then very finely chopped

30g chopped almonds, lightly toasted

Roquefort and fresh pear is a classic pairing and makes an excellent topping for a sweet/savoury pizza to serve at the end of a meal, as a cheese or dessert course. Another firm-textured blue cheese that is not too overpowering could be substituted for the Roquefort.

To make the pizza base, dissolve the yeast in the water in a small bowl. Put the remaining ingredients into the bowl of a stand mixer fitted with the dough hook, add the yeast mixture and mix for 1 minute. Using a rubber spatula, bring the dough from the sides to the middle and mix again until the dough is smooth and homogeneous. Transfer to a clean bowl, cover with cling film and leave to rise in a warm place until doubled in volume.

Preheat the oven (non-fan) to 200°C/Gas 6.

Turn the dough out onto a lightly floured surface and 'knock back', using one hand to fold the dough back in on itself until the air is knocked out and the dough is returned to its original size.

Roll out the dough on a lightly floured surface to a circle, 28cm in diameter. Flour lightly, then wrap it around the rolling pin and unravel onto a baking sheet. Using your fingertips dipped in a little flour, push the dough outwards to stretch it into a thin, even disc.

For the topping, cut the Roquefort into roughly 1cm cubes and place in a bowl. Trickle over the honey and turn gently to coat. Arrange the pieces of Roquefort evenly over the dough base.

Peel, halve and core the pears then cut into roughly 1cm pieces and place in a bowl. Spritz with the lemon juice, to prevent them discolouring, then sprinkle with the clove and mix gently. Arrange the pear on the pizza base, between the pieces of Roquefort.

Bake in the oven for 15 minutes, then scatter over the almonds and bake for a further 3 minutes. Slide the pizza onto a wire rack and leave to cool a little, for a minute or two. Cut into slices to serve.

Seafood pizza

SERVES 4

This pizza is a real feast, best served with a leafy salad that includes some peppery rocket leaves. You can, of course, introduce other seafood or fish, according to the season.

For the base

10g fresh yeast

185ml tepid water

325g 'type 55' flour, plus extra for dusting

12g fine salt

12ml extra virgin olive oil

For the topping

250g mussels

250g clams

5 medium raw prawns

100g baby squid

40ml olive oil, plus extra for oiling and the tomatoes

200g peeled plum tomatoes

40g buffalo mozzarella, broken into pieces

A few flat-leaf parsley leaves

Sea salt and freshly ground pepper

For the pizza base, dissolve the yeast in the water in a small bowl. Put the remaining ingredients into the bowl of a stand mixer fitted with the dough hook, add the yeast mixture and mix for 1 minute. Using a spatula, bring the dough from the sides to the middle and mix again until smooth. Transfer to a clean bowl, cover with cling film and leave to rise in a warm place until doubled in volume.

Turn the dough out onto a lightly floured surface and 'knock back', using one hand to fold the dough back in on itself until the air is knocked out and the dough is returned to its original size.

Steam the mussels and clams separately for 2–3 minutes until the shells open; discard any that remain closed. Remove most of them from their shells, leaving a few in their half-shells for presentation. Cook the prawns and squid on a preheated hot griddle for a few seconds, turning once, or briskly sauté in a hot oiled frying pan.

Combine the cooled shelled mussels and clams, peeled prawns and baby squid in a bowl. Trickle the olive oil over them, add a touch of salt and a generous grind of pepper, and mix gently. Set aside to marinate for 20 minutes or so.

Meanwhile, preheat the oven (non-fan) to 200°C/Gas 6. Press the tomatoes through a food mill or coarse sieve into a bowl. Season the purée with salt and pepper, and stir in a drizzle of olive oil.

Roll out the dough on a lightly floured surface to a circle, 28cm in diameter. Flour lightly, then wrap it around the rolling pin and unravel onto a baking sheet. Using your fingertips dipped in a little flour, push the dough outwards to stretch it into a thin, even disc.

Spread the puréed tomatoes over the base and bake for 20 minutes. Arrange the seafood and mozzarella evenly over the surface, then return to the oven for 2–3 minutes. Slide the pizza onto a wire rack, scatter over the parsley leaves and leave to stand for a couple of minutes before serving. Cut into wedges at the table and provide virgin olive oil for guests to add if they wish.

Calzone

Serves 2 as a main course,
4 as a starter

For the crust

10g fresh yeast

185ml tepid water

325g 'type 55' flour, plus extra
for dusting

12g fine salt

12ml light olive oil

For the filling

1 small cucumber

100ml white wine vinegar

50g caster sugar

300g ricotta

50g fines herbes (flat-leaf parsley,
chives, chervil), roughly snipped

40g basil, snipped

25g baby capers, rinsed in cold
water and dried well

12 semi-confit cherry tomatoes
(see page 248)

30g Parmigiano Reggiano, freshly
grated

Sea salt and freshly ground
pepper

Originating from Naples, a calzone is a folded pizza, usually enclosing a filling of ham or salami, ricotta and Parmesan. My version features sweet-sour cucumber, which pairs well with the ricotta. It is a fine-crusted calzone, offering plenty of filling in relation to the dough. Do give it a go.

For the crust, dissolve the yeast in the water in a small bowl. Put the remaining ingredients into the bowl of a stand mixer fitted with the dough hook, add the yeast mixture and mix for 1 minute. Using a rubber spatula, bring the dough from the sides to the middle and mix again until the dough is smooth. Transfer to a clean bowl, cover with cling film and leave to rise in a warm place until doubled in size.

For the filling, peel the cucumber, halve lengthways and scrape out the seeds, then cut into long batons and place in a bowl. Bring the wine vinegar to the boil in a pan over a medium heat and stir in the sugar. Pour over the cucumber and leave to marinate for 5 minutes. Drain the cucumber, place on a lightly dampened tea towel, cover and set aside to cool. Put the ricotta, herbs, capers and tomatoes into a bowl, season with salt and pepper and mix together gently.

Preheat the oven to 200°C/Gas 6. Turn the dough out onto a lightly floured surface and 'knock back', using one hand to fold the dough back in on itself until the air is knocked out. Roll out the dough on a lightly floured surface to a circle, 28cm in diameter. Flour lightly, then wrap it around the rolling pin and unravel onto a cold baking sheet. Using your fingertips dipped in flour, push the dough outwards to stretch it into a thin, even disc.

Sprinkle the Parmesan evenly over the dough, leaving a 5cm clear margin around the edge. Tip the ricotta and tomato mixture onto one side of the circle and brush cold water around the margin of the half without any filling. Place the cucumber batons over the filling, spacing them evenly and pushing them into the filling.

Bring the plain half of the dough over the filling and press the edges together. Pinch between your lightly floured thumb and forefinger, giving the border a quarter-turn inwards every centimetre to create a plaited effect and to seal it well. Bake for 25 minutes. Slide onto a wire rack and leave to cool for 1–2 minutes, then transfer to a board or platter and cut into portions at the table.

Vegetables

Mozzarella

Griddled aubergines and courgettes with goat's cheese

SERVES 4

1 long courgette (about 200g), trimmed

1 good, firm aubergine (about 250g), trimmed

150ml light olive oil

1 Clacbitou or other flavourful not too strong, semi-firm goat's cheese, such as Charolais, cut into rounds about 3mm thick

Sea salt and freshly ground pepper

For the tomato tartare

400g flavourful tomatoes

3 tbsp extra virgin olive oil

1 tsp thyme flowers (optional)

8 basil leaves, snipped

To finish

Extra virgin olive oil, to trickle (optional)

Small basil sprigs

This dish is easy to prepare. You can use another semi-firm goat's cheese in place of the Clacbitou if you wish – one that not too strong, otherwise it will overwhelm the flavour of the griddled vegetables. A chilled tomato tartare provides a refreshing contrast. Serve as a starter or light lunch or supper.

First prepare the tomato tartare. Immerse the tomatoes in a bowl of just-boiled water for 15 seconds or so to loosen the skins, then refresh in chilled water, remove and peel away the skins. Halve the tomatoes and scoop out the seeds then cut the flesh into small dice and place in a clean bowl. Chill in the fridge until ready to serve.

Preheat the oven to 200°C/Gas 6. Set a griddle pan over a high heat.

Using a small knife, cut the courgette and aubergine lengthways into thin slices, about 3mm thick. Brush all the slices generously with the light olive oil and sprinkle with a little salt. Cook in batches on the hot griddle pan: after 1 minute give them a quarter-turn and cook for a further minute to achieve a criss-cross charred pattern. Turn the slices over and repeat the process, giving a total of 4 minutes on the griddle, then drain on kitchen paper.

Once they are all cooked, arrange the vegetables in an ovenproof dish in alternating, overlapping layers (aubergine, goat's cheese, courgette, another goat's cheese round, then a slice of aubergine and so on). Season with pepper to taste and cook in the oven for 6 minutes until the courgette and aubergine are hot, and the edges of the goat's cheese rounds are just starting to melt.

Meanwhile, to finish the tomato tartare, stir the extra virgin olive oil into the chilled tomato dice with the thyme flowers, if available, and snipped basil. Season with salt and pepper to taste.

Serve the courgette, aubergine and goat's cheese straight from the oven dish, sprinkled with a few drops of olive oil, if you like, and garnished with basil sprigs. Serve the tomato tartare on the side.

Artichoke hearts stuffed with spinach and mushrooms

4 large Breton globe artichokes (about 300g each)

1 lemon, cut in half, plus the juice of ¼ lemon

60g butter

150g button mushrooms, wiped clean with a damp cloth and finely sliced

200g baby spinach leaves, stems removed, well washed, drained and patted dry

A generous pinch of caster sugar

250ml béchamel sauce (see page 246, ½ quantity)

80g Gruyère or Emmenthal, finely grated

Sea salt and freshly ground pepper

Fresh artichokes take some time to prepare but they are well worth the effort for this exceptional dish. For convenience, you can prepare and cook them the day before, ready to assemble with the cooked spinach and mushrooms shortly before serving. Serve the dish as a starter or vegetable side dish with grilled or barbecued meat. (Illustrated overleaf.)

Break or cut off the stems from the artichokes. Remove the outside leaves from the base of each artichoke, by holding each leaf firmly between your thumb and forefinger and twisting it towards the base of the heart. Once you have removed approximately 20 leaves from the base of each, pare each heart using a small, very sharp knife to even out the base until almost flat, and to expose the flesh.

Using a serrated knife, cut off the top part of each artichoke, about 4cm from the base, so removing the clump of leaves found in the middle of each. Using a small knife, pare around the top part of each heart again to neaten them, as for the bases. Rub each heart with one of the lemon halves to prevent them from turning brown. Immediately immerse the artichoke hearts in a bowl containing enough cold water to cover, with the juice from the lemon half (used for rubbing) added.

Bring a saucepan filled with lightly salted water to the boil. Drain the artichoke hearts and add them to the boiling water. As soon as the water returns to the boil, add the other lemon half, cut into 4 pieces. Cook the artichoke hearts over a medium heat for 30 minutes. To check that they are cooked, insert the tip of a knife into one: it should slide in without any difficulty. Transfer the artichoke hearts and their cooking water to a bowl and set aside.

Heat 20g of the butter in a small frying pan over a medium heat, add the mushrooms with a little salt and the lemon juice and cook for 1 minute. Tip into a bowl and set aside.

continued overleaf

continued from previous page

Heat the remaining butter in a large frying pan over a medium heat. Add the spinach with the sugar and a pinch of salt and cook for 2 minutes, turning it every 30 seconds with tongs or a fork. Drain well in a colander and set aside in a bowl.

Preheat the oven to 180°C/Gas 4.

Reheat the béchamel in a saucepan over a gentle heat. As soon as it is bubbling, remove from the heat and mix in the grated cheese. Set aside, covered with cling film, to keep hot.

Drain the artichoke hearts. Using your thumb or a soup spoon, remove the choke part from each heart. Grind some pepper over each artichoke, then place in an ovenproof dish.

Spoon a little cheese sauce into the base of each artichoke. Divide the spinach between the artichokes then cover with a little dome of sliced mushrooms. Spoon over some sauce to coat, but not too much; you should be able to see a few mushrooms and spinach leaves here and there.

Place the dish in the oven and bake for 8–10 minutes until the topping is lightly gratinated; if necessary, finish under a hot grill for 30 seconds. Serve straight away, with any remaining cheesy béchamel in a jug on the side.

Courgettes stuffed with Beaufort

SERVES 4

8 round courgettes
(150–200g each)

100ml light olive oil, plus extra
for oiling

2 shallots, finely chopped

Juice of 1 lemon

10g marjoram or basil, finely
snipped

220g Beaufort

Sea salt and freshly ground
pepper

Round courgettes lend themselves perfectly to stuffing with
a deeply savoury filling, as here. Beaufort is a semi-hard cow's
milk cheese, which is flavourful but not too strong. Other similar
cheeses, such as Gruyère or Comté, can be used in its place.

Cut off the top 5mm of stem attached to each courgette, then slice
off the top quarter, to create a lid. Set these lids aside.

Using a melon baller or teaspoon, scrape out the inside flesh from
the courgettes, leaving about a 5mm layer of flesh attached to the
skins. Chop the scooped-out flesh and set aside.

Heat 50ml of the olive oil in a pan over a medium heat, then add
the shallots and sweat, stirring, for 3 minutes. Add the chopped
courgette flesh, lemon juice and some salt and pepper, and cook
gently over a medium heat for 15 minutes, stirring every few minutes.
Remove from the heat and set aside to cool. Once cold, stir in your
chosen herb.

Meanwhile, preheat the oven to 200°C/Gas 6. Cut 180g of the
cheese into roughly 1.5cm cubes; finely grate the rest of the cheese
and set aside.

Sprinkle the inside of each hollowed-out courgette with salt and
pepper and spoon in the cooled filling, distributing the cubes of
cheese evenly through the mixture as you go.

Stand the filled courgettes in a lightly oiled oven dish and brush all
over with the remaining 50ml olive oil. Pour 50ml water into the dish
around (not over) the courgettes, and bake for 40 minutes.

Remove from the oven and place a reserved lid on each courgette.
Bake for a further 20 minutes, then sprinkle generously with the
grated cheese. Return to the oven for 2–3 minutes until the cheese
has melted and is cloaking the courgettes.

Serve the courgettes straight from the dish, offering two each.
Tip the cooking juices from the dish into a jug and pass it around
to pour inside the courgettes as you start to eat them.

Filo tart with Mediterranean vegetables and goat's cheese

SERVES 4

1 large onion (ideally red)

1 courgette (about 180g), trimmed

1 small, firm aubergine, trimmed

1 small green pepper, halved, cored and deseeded

1 small red pepper, halved, cored and deseeded

150ml light olive oil

1 garlic clove, cut into slivers

1 thyme sprig, leaves picked

2 small fresh goat's cheeses, each cut into 4 or 6 pieces

4 sheets of filo pastry

Sea salt and freshly ground pepper

You can vary the vegetables for this tart, according to the season and what you have to hand. Mushrooms mixed with a handful of spinach leaves are a delightful addition, for example. In summer, I add cherry tomatoes and replace the thyme with basil; I also brush the pastry base with a little black olive tapenade. Artisan cheese-makers in the Deux-Sèvres area of Poitou-Charentes produce some of the finest goat's cheeses, but France is not the only source. I have come across excellent local goat's cheeses across the globe, including the UK. Perroche from Herefordshire is one of my favourites.

Cut the onion into 8 wedges. Cut the courgette into 2cm slices and the aubergine into pieces about 1.5 x 2cm. Cut both peppers into roughly 2cm pieces.

Heat 100ml of the olive oil in a large frying pan over a medium heat. Add the aubergine and cook, stirring occasionally, for about 5 minutes, then add the onion and peppers and cook for 10 minutes, stirring every 2–3 minutes. Add the courgette and garlic and cook for a further 10 minutes, stirring. Sprinkle in the thyme and season with salt and pepper to taste.

Finally, add the pieces of goat's cheese, increase the heat and cook for another 2 minutes until the vegetables are lightly coloured and about three-quarters cooked. Transfer to a dish, cover with cling film and pierce it in several places with the tip of knife. Set aside.

Preheat the oven to 180°C/Gas 4. Brush a loose-based 18–20cm square tin, about 3.5cm deep, with some of the remaining olive oil.

Lightly brush a sheet of filo with oil and gently press it into the oiled tin. Repeat with the remaining 3 sheets of filo. Using scissors, trim off any excess pastry overhanging the edges. Fill the filo pastry case with the vegetable and cheese mixture and fold the edges of the filo inwards to form a rim. Bake for 25–30 minutes.

Slide the tin onto a wire rack and leave the tart to rest for a few minutes before removing from the tin. Serve hot, cut into squares.

Cauliflower gratin with pistou

SERVES 6

1 cauliflower (about 600g), with tight, white florets (a sign of freshness) and blemish-free

½ lemon, cut into 4 pieces

40g butter

120g Comté, Gruyère or Cheddar, coarsely grated

1 litre béchamel sauce (see page 246, double quantity)

½ quantity pistou (see page 247)

Sea salt and freshly ground pepper

Vibrant pistou introduces delightful, fragrant notes to a classic cauliflower cheese. This dish can be prepared the day before and kept in the fridge, ready to bake from chilled for about 25–30 minutes before serving.

Bring a large pan of water to the boil. Remove the outer ribs and leaves from the cauliflower then, using a small knife, split it into large florets. Trim some of the thickness from the base stem of each floret, so you keep just the tender part, then wash in cold water.

Lower the cauliflower florets into the boiling water, salt the water lightly and add the lemon pieces. Cook over a medium heat for about 12–15 minutes until the cauliflower is almost tender (i.e. still firm but not at all crunchy). To check, prod one of the stems with the tip of a sharp knife; it should slide in without much difficulty. Drain in a colander, then run under cold water for a few minutes to stop the cooking. Drain well, discard the lemon and set aside.

Preheat the oven to 190°C/Gas 5. Use the butter to generously grease a gratin dish, then sprinkle about a quarter of the grated cheese evenly over the base.

Heat the béchamel sauce in a pan over a medium heat, stirring with a balloon whisk. As soon as it comes to the boil, remove from the heat and stir in about half of the remaining grated cheese. Season with salt and pepper to taste.

Pour about one-fifth of the sauce into the gratin dish. Arrange the cauliflower florets on top, packing them against each other, then coat generously with the rest of the sauce. Sprinkle the remaining cheese evenly over the surface and bake for 20–25 minutes until the cauliflower is hot and the topping is nicely golden.

Remove from the oven and, using a teaspoon, dot generous dollops of pistou over the top, spacing them evenly. Serve the rest of the pistou separately in a jug, for guests to help themselves.

Roasted summer vegetables with goat's cheese

100ml light, fruity olive oil

6–8 garlic cloves (unpeeled)

2 medium red onions, each cut into 6 wedges

1 red pepper, cored, deseeded and cut into large pieces

1 green or yellow pepper, cored, deseeded and cut into large pieces

1 fennel bulb, trimmed and cut into small dice

1 medium aubergine, trimmed and cut into medium pieces

1 rosemary sprig, leaves stripped

12 cherry tomatoes

1 medium courgette, trimmed and cut into large cubes

1 lemon, cut into small cubes

75ml runny honey

240g young, flavourful goat's cheese

Sea salt and freshly ground pepper

15g marjoram, basil or flat-leaf parsley, roughly snipped, to finish

For this delightful ensemble, I like to use a relatively young, flavourful goat's cheese, such as Monte Enebro with a natural rind (cut into small pieces), or a ripened Bauma Carrat or soft, washed-rind Aravis Chevrotin (cut into large pieces). These are from different countries – there are no borders when it comes to cheese – they are particular favourites, but you can use any goat's cheese here. Any leftover roasted vegetables will be delicious the next day as an omelette filling.

Preheat the oven to 190°C/Gas 5.

Heat the olive oil in a very large frying pan or wide sauté pan over a medium heat. Add the garlic cloves and onion wedges and cook for 3 minutes, then add the peppers, fennel and aubergine. Cook for 5 minutes, stirring every minute or two.

Add the rosemary, cherry tomatoes, courgette and lemon. Season lightly with salt and cook for a further 5 minutes, stirring every minute or two.

Transfer all the vegetables to a roasting tin or dish (if your pan is not ovenproof) and cook in the oven for 15 minutes. Stir the vegetables then drizzle over the honey. Distribute the pieces of goat's cheese evenly on top, burying them slightly into the vegetables. Return to the oven for another 20 minutes.

Transfer the roasted vegetables and cheese to a serving dish, add a light grinding of pepper and sprinkle over your chosen aromatic herb. Serve hot.

Malfatti on a red pepper and tomato coulis

SERVES 6

350g young spinach leaves, stalks removed, well washed

1 medium onion, finely chopped

20ml light olive oil

1 garlic clove, chopped

280g ricotta

2 medium eggs

300g fine breadcrumbs

40g plain flour

A pinch of freshly grated nutmeg

50g Parmigiano Reggiano, finely grated

40g butter

Sea salt and freshly ground pepper

For the pepper and tomato coulis

3 red peppers

20ml light olive oil, for brushing

1 tbsp extra virgin olive oil

1 medium onion, finely chopped

100ml cold water

2 savory or thyme sprigs

200g tomatoes, peeled, deseeded and diced

Basil leaves, to finish

The pillowy softness of ricotta and the vibrancy of spinach come together in these gnocchi-like quenelles, which are perfectly offset by a fresh-tasting coulis. A great Italian classic.

First, make the coulis. Heat up a ridged griddle pan over a high heat (or preheat an oven grill to high). Quarter the peppers lengthways and remove the stalks, core and seeds. Brush the skin side with light olive oil. Lay skin side down on the hot griddle (or under the grill) until the skin is charred and blistered. Remove and briefly immerse in iced water to cool, then peel away the skin. Set aside in a colander.

Heat the extra virgin olive oil in a pan, add the onion and soften for 1 minute, then add the peppers, water and savory or thyme and simmer for 5 minutes. Transfer to a blender and blitz for 1 minute. Season with salt and pepper to taste. Strain the pepper coulis through a chinois into a small pan; keep hot.

For the malfatti, blanch the spinach in boiling water for 1 minute. Drain, refresh in cold water, then drain again and squeeze between your hands to remove as much water as possible. Chop the spinach finely and put into a large bowl. Add the onion and light olive oil, the garlic, ricotta, eggs and breadcrumbs. Mix with a wooden spoon until thoroughly combined. Add some salt and pepper and then add the flour, nutmeg and half the Parmesan and mix well again.

Using 2 soup spoons, shape the mixture into 12 quenelles and place on a tray lined with greaseproof paper. Chill for 20–30 minutes.

You will need to cook the malfatti in batches. Heat a pan of lightly salted water to 70–80°C (below a simmer). Drop in 3 or 4 malfatti at a time and poach for 5 minutes until they float to the surface. Remove with a skimmer and drain well. Repeat to poach the rest.

Melt the butter in a large frying pan over a medium heat until hot but not bubbling. Add the malfatti and gently turn through the butter for 1–2 minutes. Mix the diced tomatoes into the hot pepper coulis and spread over the base of a wide serving dish. Arrange the malfatti on top, garnish with the basil leaves and serve, handing the remaining grated Parmesan around separately.

Roasted peppers with halloumi

2 yellow peppers

2 red peppers

80ml light olive oil

A generous pinch of soft
brown sugar

200g tomatoes, peeled, cut in
half horizontally and deseeded

3 thyme sprigs

2 bay leaves

2 garlic cloves, peeled and bashed

Grapeseed oil, for deep-frying

120g fine breadcrumbs

3 tsp cayenne pepper or 5 tsp
smoked paprika

250g halloumi, cut into about
1.5cm cubes

Sea salt and freshly ground
pepper

A small handful of coriander
sprigs, to finish

A dish of Cypriot, Greek and Turkish resonance, with dazzling colours and mouth-watering flavours. This is a delicious way of cooking halloumi, providing the bonbons are served good and hot. I have a slight preference for the cayenne breadcrumbs over smoked paprika, but the choice is yours.

Preheat the oven to 200°C/Gas 6.

Using a small knife, cut out the stalk ends off the 4 peppers, to create an opening, then use a knife to remove the core and seeds from inside, without opening up the peppers.

Heat up a ridged griddle pan over a high heat. Brush the outsides of each pepper with a little of the olive oil and season the insides lightly with salt. Cook on the griddle pan, turning as necessary, until lightly marked all the way around. Transfer to a roasting dish and roast in the oven for about 20 minutes until cooked but still just retaining their shape.

Meanwhile, heat a large frying pan or sauté pan over a high heat and add 50ml of the olive oil. When it is hot, add the sugar then immediately place the halved tomatoes in the pan, cut side down, and add the thyme, bay leaves and garlic. Season with a little salt and a generous grinding of pepper. Cook, without moving the tomatoes too much, for 5 minutes. Spoon the contents of the pan over the base of a wide serving dish; keep warm.

Heat the oil for deep-frying in a deep-fryer or other deep, heavy pan to 180°C. Mix the breadcrumbs with the cayenne or paprika. Roll the cubes of halloumi, 6 or 8 at a time, in the crumb mixture to coat all over, and pat with your hands to make sure it adheres well. Drop into the hot oil and cook for about 1 minute until they turn golden brown. Remove with a skimmer and drain on kitchen paper. Repeat to coat and fry the remaining halloumi cubes.

To serve, arrange the roasted peppers, open side up, on top of the tomato base and fill the cavity of each with the halloumi bonbons, keeping some back to scatter here and there on top of the tomato base. Garnish with the coriander and serve at once.

Cheesy potato and turnip gratin

Serves 4-6

350g medium waxy potatoes, such as Charlotte or Bintje

200g turnips

400ml double cream

50ml milk

A knifetip of freshly grated nutmeg

150g Hafod hard cheese, or a young, firm Comté, grated

1 small garlic clove, halved

Sea salt and freshly ground pepper

This is a lovely gratin to serve with roast chicken, lamb or beef and it reheats beautifully in the oven at 120°C/Gas ½ if you have any left over. You could use an alternative hard or semi-hard cheese, such as Cheddar or Gruyère, if you like.

Preheat the oven to 160°C/Gas 3.

Peel and wash the potatoes, then cut into fine slices, 2–3mm thick. Spread the slices out on your work surface, sprinkle generously with salt and rub together well. Gather them into a heap and leave to stand for 10 minutes.

Peel the turnips, then wash and cut into fine slices, 3–4mm thick. Season lightly with salt, rub together well, then gather into a heap and leave for about 5 minutes.

Pour the cream and milk into a large pan and place over a medium heat. Add the nutmeg and a grinding of pepper and heat gently. As soon as it is warm, take small handfuls of the potato slices and squeeze out all the water, then add to the cream mixture. Repeat with the turnips.

Gently mix the potatoes and turnips into the cream mixture and bring to the boil, still over a medium heat. Cook, stirring, for 1–2 minutes, then remove from the heat and mix in the grated cheese.

Rub the inside of a gratin dish with the cut garlic clove, dipping it from time to time into salt. Pour the potato and turnip mixture into the dish and spread it out into an even layer. Bake in the oven for 45 minutes until tender and golden brown on the surface.

Leave the gratin to stand in a warm place for 15–20 minutes. Serve straight from the dish or, if you prefer, cut out individual portions using a 5–7cm plain cutter.

Aligot

1.25kg floury potatoes, such as Maris Piper or King Edward

250ml crème fraîche

250ml milk

125g butter, cut into small pieces

400–500g Tomme fraîche de l'Aubrac cheese, cut into very small pieces

Sea salt and freshly ground pepper

This rustic, potato purée from the Auvergne region of France is divine. Tomme fraîche de l'Aubrac is traditionally used but hard to find; Swiss Appenzeller is a good substitute. The amount of cheese you need will depend on the finished weight of the purée, so buy extra to make sure you have enough. To take this dish to another level, fry small back fat dice until lightly golden then tip it over the aligot as you serve.

Peel the potatoes and wash in cold water, then place in a saucepan and cover with lightly salted cold water. Bring to the boil and cook over a medium heat until tender when tested with the tip of a knife.

Just before the potatoes are cooked, put the crème fraîche and milk into a pan and bring to the boil, then strain through a fine chinois into a bowl.

You will need to weigh the purée before you add the cheese, so either put the pan you are using on the scales so you can calculate the weight of the purée once made, or have a warmed bowl ready to tip the mixture into for weighing.

Drain the potatoes thoroughly and pass through a potato ricer or a mouli on the finest setting, into the pan. Using a wooden spoon, incorporate the butter a little at a time into the hot potato, then gradually beat in the very hot crème fraîche and milk mixture. It should be at 60–64°C.

Calculate the weight of the purée at this stage, then measure out 80g cheese for every 200g purée.

Put the pan over a low heat and, using a wooden spoon, gradually incorporate the pieces of cheese. Work the mixture well; the purée will become smoother and more elastic, eventually turning stringy when you lift it up with the spoon. Check the seasoning, adding plenty of pepper (the cheese provides enough salt).

Transfer the aligot to a warmed dish to serve. If necessary, it can be kept warm in a bain-marie for 10–15 minutes, but after this it will start to lose its heat and character.

Dauphine potatoes with Emmenthal

SERVES 4–6

400g floury potatoes, such as Maris Piper or King Edward

About 1.5 litres grapeseed oil, for deep-frying

For the choux pastry

70ml milk

70ml water

50g butter, cut into dice

A pinch of freshly grated nutmeg

A pinch of sea salt

3 turns of the pepper mill

100g plain flour

2 medium eggs

50g Emmenthal (or Comté), finely grated

Not to be confused with Potato Dauphinoise – the more familiar, classic potato bake – these potato croquettes have a light choux pastry base. Appetising and flavoursome, they are particularly good served with my grilled halibut steak with Parmesan and ginger hollandaise (see page 123).

First make the choux paste. Put the milk, water, butter, nutmeg, salt and pepper into a saucepan and place over a low heat. Bring to the boil then immediately take the pan off the heat and shower in the flour, mixing as you do so with a wooden spoon until smooth.

Return the pan to a medium heat and stir for a minute or so to dry the paste, then tip it into a large bowl. Add the eggs one at a time, beating well between each addition, then mix in the cheese. The paste should be smooth and shiny. Cover with cling film; set aside.

Peel the potatoes and wash in cold water, then place in a saucepan and cover with lightly salted cold water. Bring to the boil and cook over a medium heat until tender when tested with the tip of a knife. Drain well and pass through a potato ricer or fine sieve into a bowl. Cover the bowl with cling film and set aside.

Once the potato is at roughly the same temperature as the choux pastry (ideally just warm), weigh the choux and mix an equal weight of potato into it. This can be done using an electric mixer fitted with the paddle attachment, or by hand with a wooden spoon. The resulting mixture must be perfectly homogeneous and smooth, without any trace of unmixed potato or choux.

Heat the oil for deep-frying in a deep-fryer or other suitable deep, heavy pan to 180°C. Using 2 teaspoons or dessertspoons, shape 18–24 quenelles from the mixture, placing them on a sheet of very lightly oiled greaseproof paper.

You will need to cook in batches, One by one, lower 6–8 quenelles into the hot oil, using a small palette knife. After 2–3 minutes, when they have taken on a light brown colour and float up to the surface, remove using a skimmer, and place on kitchen paper to drain well for a minute. Repeat with the remaining quenelles.

Pile the dauphine potatoes into a warmed dish and serve at once.

Great Classics

Gruyère

Parmesan soufflés

SERVES 8

Don't be afraid of making soufflés, they are easier to master than you might think. My advice is to be bold and just go for it. The variations suggested below are all delicious, but this Parmesan version is certainly the lightest of them all.

For the dishes

75g butter, softened

50g Parmesan, freshly grated

For the soufflés

40g butter

40g plain flour

500ml cold milk

2 pinches of cayenne pepper

10 medium free-range eggs, plus an extra 2 yolks

180g Parmigiano Reggiano, freshly grated

Sea salt and freshly ground pepper

For Cheddar soufflés, replace the Parmesan in the soufflé mixture with 200g Cheddar and use 80g for lining the dishes. For Gruyère or Comté soufflés, use 240g cheese for the mixture, and 80g for the dishes.

Generously grease 8 individual soufflé dishes, 10cm in diameter and 6cm tall, using the softened butter. Add the grated Parmesan to one of the buttered dishes, then rotate the dish, tilting it over a second dish so that you coat the insides of the first dish and the excess drops into the second. Repeat this process with the remaining dishes until they are all coated.

To prepare the soufflés, melt the butter in a small pan. Add the flour and cook, stirring with a small balloon whisk, for 2 minutes to make a roux. Gradually stir in the cold milk and, still stirring with the whisk, bring to the boil over a medium heat. Simmer for 1 minute, then pour the béchamel into a bowl. Add a little salt and pepper and the cayenne, then whisk in the 12 egg yolks. Cover with cling film and set aside in a warm place.

Preheat the oven to 200°C/Gas 6. In a very clean bowl, whisk the egg whites with a pinch of salt to semi-firm peaks. Without delay, whisk one-third of the whites into the warm béchamel. Now, using a spatula or large spoon, very gently fold in the rest of the whites, while showering in the grated Parmesan with your other hand; stop mixing as soon as the mixture is just combined.

Using a spoon, generously fill the dishes to 1.5cm above the rim. Gently smooth the tops using a small palette knife, then run the tip of a knife around the inside of each dish to detach the mixture from the side and allow for a good rise.

Line the base of a roasting tray with baking parchment and stand the soufflé dishes in the tray. Pour near-boiling water from the kettle into the tray to come halfway up the side of the soufflé dishes and bake in the oven for 8 minutes.

Remove from the oven and lift the soufflé dishes out onto warmed plates. Serve immediately... they don't like to sit around.

Soufflés Suissesse

SERVES 8 AS A STARTER; 4 AS A LUNCH

140g butter, softened

65g 'type 55' flour

700ml cold milk

5 medium eggs, separated, plus 1 extra egg white

750ml double cream

200g Gruyère or Emmenthal, freshly grated

Sea salt and freshly ground pepper

Cheddar also works very well in place of Gruyère or Emmenthal.

This soufflé was our speciality when Albert, my brother, and I opened our restaurant Le Gavroche in 1967. It has survived passing trends and still features on the menu there. Albert was a great expert in pulling off this delicious, feathery-light dish that has a hint of richness to it. To try it is to love it…

Place 8 plain tartlet moulds, 8cm in diameter and 1.5cm deep, in the fridge to chill.

Melt 65g of the butter in a saucepan over a low heat. Add the flour and cook, stirring, with a small balloon whisk, for 2 minutes. Gradually stir in the cold milk, then bring to the boil over a medium heat, still stirring with the whisk to keep the mixture smooth. Simmer for 2 minutes, then remove from the heat and whisk in the egg yolks. Dot 20g of the remaining butter over the surface to prevent a skin forming, cover with cling film and set aside.

Preheat the oven to 220°C/Gas 7. Take the tartlet moulds from the fridge and butter the insides very generously, using the remaining butter and your finger to apply it. Place them on a baking tray.

Pour the cream into a large, shallow ovenproof dish. Season lightly with salt and a generous grinding of pepper. Place over a low heat.

Using an electric whisk, whisk the 6 egg whites with a good pinch of salt to soft peaks. Transfer the soufflé mixture to a large, wide bowl. Swiftly incorporate one-third of the whisked egg whites into the mixture, using a balloon whisk, then carefully fold in the remaining whites with a rubber spatula.

Using a large spoon, spoon the mixture in mounds into the prepared moulds, dividing it equally. Immediately place in the oven and bake for 3 minutes until the tops start to turn pale blond.

Using a tea towel to protect your hand, remove from the oven and quickly turn each soufflé out into the dish of warmed cream. Sprinkle the cheese over the soufflés and bake for a further 4–5 minutes.

Serve at once, presenting the floating soufflés at the table in their dish of cream. Using a large spoon and a fork, serve one or two each, basting a little cream over each.

Omelette with Gruyère and caviar

SERVES 2

6 medium eggs, at room temperature

20g clarified butter or grapeseed oil

80g semi-dry, slightly aged, goat's cheese, coarsely grated

50ml double cream

60g Gruyère (aged for 6–12 months), finely grated

50g very fresh Sevruga or Beluga caviar, well chilled

Sea salt and freshly ground pepper

Cheese and eggs are the perfect marriage, with caviar adding the crowning touch here. Omelettes, like soufflés, need to be eaten as soon as they are cooked. I prefer a soft-set, almost runny (*baveuse*), omelette.

Preheat the grill to high.

In a bowl, beat the eggs lightly with a fork, season sparingly with salt and add a generous grinding of pepper.

Place a 20cm heavy-based frying pan, preferably non-stick, over a high heat. When it is very hot, add the clarified butter or oil, then after 5 seconds pour in the beaten eggs. Cook, without stirring, for 5–10 seconds, to allow them enough time to set just very lightly on the bottom.

Now, using the side of a fork, bring the set edges of the egg towards the middle and stir constantly, lightly shaking the pan with your other hand, until the eggs are cooked to your liking: about 1 minute for quite runny; 1 minute, 20 seconds for medium (*à point*); and 2 minutes for well done.

Sprinkle the grated goat's cheese over the surface of the omelette. Now, with a sharp flick of the wrist towards you and with the pan at a slight tilt away from you, begin to roll the omelette over itself into a fold, then finish the folding by rolling it out neatly onto a warmed flameproof serving plate.

Immediately mix the cream and Gruyère together, add a generous grinding of pepper then spoon the mixture over the just-cooked omelette. Place under the grill for 20–30 seconds until it has taken on a nice golden colour.

Bring the omelette to the table and shape 2 quenelles from the caviar using 2 large spoons. Place on top of the omelette at an angle and wait for your guest's accolade.

Gruyère and Vacherin fondue

SERVES 4

1 garlic clove, peeled

400g Gruyère

400g Vacherin Fribourgeois

15g cornflour or potato flour

300ml dry white wine, ideally
a Swiss Fendant du Valais (Wallis)

A knifetip of finely, freshly grated
nutmeg

50ml kirsch (optional)

1 large crusty baguette, cut into
large dice

Sea salt and freshly ground
pepper

*The fondue burner must be set
to low and have an adjustable heat
setting, so that the temperature
of the fondue can be controlled.*

The variety of cheeses you can use for this recipe is almost infinite: Tomme de Savoie, Emmenthal Savoyard, Basque Tommette, Tomme de Béarn, Manchego, Farmhouse Cheddar, young Gouda and, of course, the marvellous Swiss cheeses Gruyère and Vacherin Fribourgeois suggested here. Alongside the baguette cubes, you can serve small new potatoes – steamed whole in their skins for about 20 minutes, then halved – to dip into the fondue, just like the bread.

Rub the garlic clove around the inside of a fondue pot or heavy pan (ideally enamelled), dipping it from time to time in salt so that it sticks well to the surface. Coarsely grate the cheeses.

Mix the cornflour or potato flour with about 50ml of the wine until smoothly blended. Add the grated cheeses to the pot, pour in the remaining wine and add the cornflour or potato flour mixture.

Place the pot over a low heat and stir frequently with a wooden spoon until the cheeses melt. As soon as they do, stir constantly, adding the nutmeg and a little pepper, to taste. As the fondue comes to the boil, add the kirsch, if using, and make sure your guests are seated and ready.

To serve, place the pot on a fondue burner or portable spirit burner in the middle of the table. Using long forks, each guest spears one piece of bread at a time with the fork and dips and turns it in the fondue before eating.

Raclette Valaisanne

SERVES 8–12

½ Valais AOP Raclette wheel (about 2.5kg), made with unpasteurised milk

1–1.5kg Raclette, Charlotte or other waxy potatoes

250g baby cornichons

250g pickled baby white onions

Sea salt and freshly ground pepper

Raclette is a great dish to share with friends. In Switzerland, dried cured meats, such as ham, beef, bacon and sausage, are often served before Raclette, with rye bread and butter. The traditional accompaniments are cornichons and pickled baby onions, plus white wine, of course, ideally Swiss Fendant du Valais. You should allow for at least six small plates of Raclette per person. It's a substantial main dish so you won't need a dessert – just offer a piece of fruit or, even better, a glass of eau de vie such as abricotine.

Be warned that the person in charge of the Raclette cannot pause at any point and must keep going until all the guests are replete!

Scrape the surface of the Raclette crust with a knife and set the cheese aside.

Wash the potatoes and cook them in their skins in lightly salted water until just tender. Take the pan off the heat and set aside to keep the potatoes warm in their cooking water until ready to serve.

Switch on and heat your electric or gas Raclette grill. Drain the potatoes and tip them into a serving dish. Have the serving plates warm and ready.

Position the half wheel of cheese on the support, with the cut side facing the hot element, about 6–8cm away from it. Heat the cheese for about 2–3 minutes until it begins to wrinkle and crease on the surface. As soon as it does, with the aid of a tea towel, slide the support that the cheese is resting on to the side of the grill, then tilt it to a 45° angle and, using the back of a knife, scrape across the bubbling hot cheese and let it slide onto a guest's plate.

Serve at once to that guest, who can eat the melted cheese with a potato or two – skin on or peeled, as preferred – lightly peppered, and with or without a cornichon and some baby onions. Repeat for the next guest.

Between every 2 Raclettes, you will need to use the blade of a very sharp knife to cut off the edge of the outside crust of the cheese, so it is flush with the cheese inside. Offer around this little crust (called the *religieuse*); it's crisp and delicious alongside the Raclette.

Spinach and cheese quiche

SERVES 6–8

300g flan pastry (see page 249)

Plain flour, for dusting

Butter, for greasing

For the filling

250g leaf spinach, well washed, stems removed

2 medium eggs, plus 4 extra egg yolks

400ml double cream

10g dill leaves, snipped

150g Comté (aged for 6–12 months), freshly grated

Sea salt and freshly ground pepper

You can use pretty much any cheese for this lovely savoury quiche. I have had excellent results with Asagio, Fontina, feta, Shipcord and various goat's cheeses, for example. I sometimes add a few diced anchovy fillets in oil to the filling too… delicious.

Roll out the pastry on a lightly floured surface to a circle, about 3mm thick. Lightly butter a 22cm tart ring, 3cm deep, and place on a baking sheet. Loosely wrap the pastry around the rolling pin and unfurl it gently over the tart ring, making sure it keeps its shape.

Using your thumb and forefinger, press the pastry against the side of the ring, starting at the base and working up towards the top. If necessary, remove any pastry overhanging the rim by rolling the rolling pin over the top of the ring, then press the pastry up against the side again and into a smooth, even ridge. Chill in the fridge to rest for 20 minutes.

Preheat the oven to 200°C/Gas 6. Prick the pastry base with a fork in 6 or 8 places, then line with a piece of baking parchment. Fill with a layer of ceramic baking beans, rice or dried beans or lentils, and bake 'blind' for 20 minutes.

Meanwhile, for the filling, add the spinach to a pan of boiling salted water and blanch for 2 minutes, then drain and refresh in cold water. Drain thoroughly and squeeze dry. Whisk the whole eggs and extra yolks together in a bowl. Add the cream and dill, and season to taste with salt and pepper.

When the part-baked pastry case is ready, carefully remove the beans and paper, then set aside to cool slightly.

Roughly chop the cooked spinach and place in a bowl with the grated cheese. Pour on the egg and cream mixture and stir with a wooden spoon until evenly combined; do not over-mix. Spoon the filling into the pastry case to come to the top of the pastry ring and bake in the oven, still at 200°C/Gas 6, for 35 minutes.

Remove from the oven and immediately slide the tart onto a wire rack. Let cool slightly for 5–10 minutes, then remove the pastry ring and serve.

Cheese Charlotte

SERVES 6

60g butter

1 baguette

400g Morbier cheese, crust removed, cut into fine slivers

6 medium eggs

A generous pinch of paprika

A pinch of freshly grated nutmeg

1 litre boiling milk

Sea salt and freshly ground pepper

150g rocket or watercress leaves, to serve (optional)

Quick and easy to make, this homely dish is always a crowd pleaser. I sometimes add a few diced anchovy fillets in oil between the layers of bread and cheese. The Morbier can be replaced with another characterful semi-soft cheese, such as Port-Salut, Emmenthal or a Swiss Raclette.

Use half the butter to grease the inside of a soufflé dish or an ovenproof Charlotte dish, 16–18cm in diameter and 10cm deep.

Cut the baguette into fine slices. Line the base of the prepared dish with a layer of bread slices, pressed tightly against each other, then arrange a layer of cheese slices over the bread. Add another layer of bread slices and continue layering in this way until the dish is full, finishing with a layer of bread. (Depending on the size of your baguette, you may have some left over.)

Preheat the oven to 200°C/Gas 6.

In a bowl, beat the eggs lightly with a fork and season very lightly with salt. Add a grinding of pepper, the paprika and nutmeg. Pour on the boiling milk, a little at a time, whisking with the fork as you do so. Pour this mixture over the bread and cheese in the dish and leave to soak in for 10 minutes.

Press down lightly on the top layer of bread with your fingertips or the back of a spoon, then dot the remaining 30g butter over the surface. Bake for 40 minutes, then check to see if it is cooked by inserting a skewer or a sharp, thin knifetip into the middle: if it comes out shiny and clean with no trace of mixture sticking to it, the Charlotte is ready. If not, continue to cook for a few more minutes.

Remove from the oven, place the dish on a wire rack and leave to stand for 2–3 minutes before serving. Take the dish to the table and use a large spoon to serve it to your guests. Offer a salad of rocket leaves or watercress on the side, if you like.

Aletsch cheese tartiflette

SERVES 4

400g small new potatoes

200g unsmoked salted pork belly, cut into fat lardons

100ml groundnut oil

1 large onion (about 200g), cut into small dice

200g button mushrooms, quartered

Juice of ¼ lemon

20g butter

50ml crème fraîche

200g Aletsch cheese, cut into strips about 3mm thick

Sea salt and freshly ground pepper

I adore this rustic, wintry dish so much that I often double up the recipe, to ensure there is the opportunity to have seconds. Any semi-soft cheese, such as Reblochon, can be substituted for Aletsch, but the Swiss mountain cheese is my favourite. Take care when eating, as the cheese will be very hot.

Wash the potatoes in their skins, then cut into large dice and dry well; set aside. Add the lardons to a pan of boiling water and blanch for 1 minute, then drain and dry well.

Heat 50ml of the oil in a frying pan over a medium heat, add the potatoes and cook, stirring every minute or so, until lightly golden all over, adding the onion to the pan when the potatoes are almost cooked through. Once cooked, set aside in a bowl.

Add the lardons and the remaining oil to the frying pan and cook, stirring, for 2–3 minutes until golden, then transfer with a slotted spoon to the bowl with the potatoes and onion; discard the oil.

Preheat the oven to 180°C/Gas 4.

Put the button mushrooms into a small pan and add the lemon juice, butter and a little splash of cold water. Bring to the boil and let bubble for 30 seconds, then drain the mushrooms.

Toss the mushrooms into the potato, onion and lardon mixture, add the crème fraîche and mix well. Add just a touch of salt and a generous grinding of pepper.

Divide the mixture between 4 small ovenproof dishes (earthenware or enamelled ceramic), about 15cm in diameter and 3cm deep. Cook in the oven for 3 minutes, then lay the strips of cheese on top and return to the oven for a further 4–5 minutes.

Serve the tartiflette straight from the oven. The cheese will have partially melted and mingled with the other elements of the dish.

Gnudi

SERVES 8-10

30ml extra virgin olive oil

700g spinach leaves, stalks removed, washed and well drained

1 garlic clove, peeled and halved

350g ricotta (sheep's or cow's), well drained

80g Parmigiano Reggiano, freshly grated

1 medium egg

50g 'type 00' flour, plus extra for dusting

Freshly grated nutmeg, to taste

150g butter

2 or 3 sage sprigs

Fine sea salt and coarsely ground black pepper

For the fried sage garnish

A bunch of sage, leaves stripped from the stalks, rinsed and drained

A little grapeseed oil, for frying

This is a fine, delicate dish of light ricotta and spinach dumplings, originating from Florence. Once shaped, the quenelles can be kept in the fridge for 24 hours before cooking, so you can make them a day ahead. Once cooked, however, they must be served at once and eaten without delay, as with a soufflé.

Heat half the olive oil in a large frying pan over a medium heat. When it is hot, add half the spinach, put the lid on and cook for 2–3 minutes, stirring every 30 seconds with a fork onto which you have pronged a half garlic clove. Once cooked, tip into a colander placed over a bowl.

Repeat to cook the rest of the spinach, using the remaining oil and the other half garlic clove, then set aside in the colander to cool.

As soon as the spinach has cooled, tip it into a very fine chinois and press down on it with a plastic spatula or the back of a spoon, to extract as much water as possible. Tip the spinach onto a board and chop roughly (though if using baby leaves, this won't be necessary).

Put the ricotta and spinach into a bowl and mix well with a wooden spoon. Shower in 50g of the Parmesan, then add the egg and shower in the flour. Mix until well combined and season with salt, pepper and nutmeg to taste.

Using 2 large spoons, shape the mixture into quenelles, about 30g each. To do this, take a heaped spoonful of the mixture and pass it repeatedly between the spoons, turning and smoothing the sides as you do so, then carefully place on a generously floured sheet of baking parchment or greaseproof paper. You should have about 36 in total. Dust with a little flour, cover loosely with cling film and set aside in a cool place until ready to cook.

To cook the gnudi, fill a large pan with water, add salt and bring to the boil. Add the quenelles to the water and poach at a bare simmer (the water should be at 80–90°C) until they rise to the surface, which indicates that they are cooked; this will take about 5 minutes. Carefully lift out the gnudi using a slotted spoon and drain, then gently place on a clean tea towel.

continued overleaf

continued from previous page

For the garnish, pat the sage leaves thoroughly dry. Heat a little grapeseed oil in a frying pan, then fry the sage leaves in batches (6–8 at a time) for about 5 seconds. Remove and drain on kitchen paper; the leaves will crisp up as they cool.

To finish the gnudi, have your warmed serving plates ready. Heat the butter with the sage sprigs in a large frying pan. As the butter starts to foam and take on a nutty brown colour, add the gnudi, making sure they are not too close together. Cook for 1 minute, then carefully turn them over and cook on the other side for a further minute.

Place 3 gnudi on each warmed plate. Arrange the fried sage leaves around the gnudi, dust with the remaining 30g Parmesan and serve.

Coulommiers with black truffle

SERVES 4–6

1 soft, but not runny, Coulommiers (about 250g), made with unpasteurised milk

50g mascarpone

2 tsp whipping cream

1 fresh black truffle (30–40g), brushed, wiped with a damp cloth and dried

Freshly ground pepper

This should be served on its own, as the single cheese in a cheese course. The flavour is so exquisite that no other cheese will be able to shine by its side. The success of this recipe lies in the quality of the cheese and the black truffle, which must be perfectly fresh and at the peak of its season. The same technique can be applied to an unpasteurised wheel of Brie, which will serve between 30 and 40 guests.

Split the Coulommiers in half horizontally, using a very sharp or serrated knife. Mix the mascarpone with the whipping cream. Using a palette knife, spread the mascarpone and cream mixture over both cut sides of the cheese and add a light grinding of pepper.

Using a small truffle mandoline or swivel peeler, very lightly peel the truffle, then shave the entire truffle over a bowl into slivers, about 1mm thick.

Starting at the outside edge of the bottom half of the Coulommiers and overhanging the edge by about 2mm, arrange the truffle slices in a rosette, working towards the middle until the entire surface is covered in truffle. Add a turn of the pepper mill and add a second layer of truffle over the first layer, using the same method.

Place the top half of the cheese over the truffle-covered base, to reform the cheese to its original shape. Lightly press down on the cheese with your fingertips, then wrap in cling film and place in the least-cold part of the fridge for at least 24 hours, and up to 48 hours, to infuse with the truffle.

Remove the cheese from the fridge at least 1 or 2 hours before serving. Cut into 4 or 6 portions at the table – the aromas released play a part in the pleasure and anticipation of eating the cheese. I recommend serving it with plain bread, artisanal if possible.

Desserts

Ricotta

Panna cotta with poached rhubarb

For the panna cotta

3½ sheets of leaf gelatine

250ml milk

130g caster sugar

2 vanilla pods (ideally Bourbon),
split in half lengthways

680g fromage frais, at room
temperature

6 tiny mint sprigs

For the poached rhubarb

80g caster sugar

150ml cold water

180g young, tender rhubarb stems

For a lighter panna cotta, fromage frais replaces the usual cream, and lightly poached rhubarb provides a lovely contrast to the silky texture. The panna cotta can be made a day in advance, which is convenient if you are entertaining.

For the panna cotta, soak the gelatine in a shallow dish of cold water for 5 minutes.

Put the milk, sugar and vanilla pods into a saucepan and place over a medium heat. As soon as it comes to the boil, remove from the heat. Immediately drain the gelatine, squeeze out excess water, then add to the hot milk, stirring with a whisk to dissolve.

Put the fromage frais into a food processor or blender. Remove the vanilla pods from the milk and, using the back of a small knife, scrape out the seeds and return them to the milk; discard the pods.

With the processor or blender on a low speed, slowly pour the hot, vanilla-infused milk onto the fromage frais then, once it is all added, increase the speed to medium and process for 1 minute until smooth. Strain through a fine chinois into a bowl.

Set the bowl over a larger bowl of iced water to cool the mixture quickly, stirring from time to time. When it is almost cold, divide between 6 panna cotta or dariole moulds, about 8cm diameter and 5cm deep. Refrigerate for at least 3–4 hours.

For the poached rhubarb, dissolve the sugar in the water in a pan over a medium heat and bring to the boil. Meanwhile, peel the rhubarb stems with a swivel peeler, then cut into fairly large julienne and lower them into the boiling sugar syrup. Poach at a low simmer for 30 seconds, then tip the rhubarb and syrup into a bowl. Set aside to cool, then refrigerate until ready to serve.

To serve, dip the base of a panna cotta mould into a bowl filled with just-boiled water for 10 seconds. Invert a plate over the mould then, holding them firmly together, turn over to unmould the panna cotta onto the plate. Repeat with the rest of the moulds.

Spoon the rhubarb around the panna cotta and pour a little of the syrup over it. Finish each panna cotta with a mint sprig and serve.

Tiramisu verrine

SERVES 4–6

3 egg yolks

60g caster sugar

200g mascarpone

200ml whipping cream

50g icing sugar

3 very strong shots of espresso, cooled

1 tbsp sambuca

6 large, soft, fluffy sponge fingers (bought from a pâtisserie)

30g dark, unsweetened cocoa powder, sifted

16 coffee beans, roughly crushed

I like to serve this classic dessert in individual glasses for an elegant presentation. The crushed coffee beans add a surprise crunch that works perfectly with the tiramisu's smooth, creamy texture.

Put the egg yolks and caster sugar into a small bowl and whisk until the mixture is pale, creamy and thick enough to leave a ribbon when the whisk is lifted. Add the mascarpone and fold through until evenly combined.

In another bowl, whip the cream with the icing sugar until softly peaking. Using a spatula, carefully fold the two mixtures together until smoothly combined; avoid overworking.

Mix the cold espresso shots with the sambuca in a shallow dish, just large enough to fit the sponge fingers. Add the sponge fingers to the dish and turn them over after 30 seconds so that they are evenly soaked.

Divide about one-fifth of the creamy mixture between 4–6 cocktail glasses, then gently place a layer of soaked sponge on top (using just over one-third of them). Spoon another layer of the creamy mixture on top, then arrange the remaining sponge over the surface. Spoon the rest of the creamy mixture on top. Refrigerate for at least 3 hours before serving.

To finish, from a piece of card large enough to cover the top of each serving glass, cut out a circle, about 3cm in diameter, from the middle, to make a neat hole. Sit the cardboard on the rim of one glass, making sure that the hole is in the middle, then generously sprinkle cocoa into the middle. Remove the card and repeat with the remaining tiramisu glasses.

Sprinkle the crushed coffee beans around the edge of each tiramisu and serve very cold.

Mascarpone-stuffed poached apricots

SERVES 6

18–24 ready-to-eat dried apricots (depending on size)

300g caster sugar

600ml water

300g mascarpone

1 vanilla pod (ideally Bourbon), or a few drops of vanilla extract

60g blanched pistachio nuts, roughly chopped

I came across this dessert recently when some friends invited me over for dinner. It is truly delicious, yet quick and easy to prepare. You need good-quality succulent dried apricots; serve 3–4 per person.

Carefully slit the dried apricots along one side to create an opening.

Dissolve the sugar in the water in a pan over a medium heat and bring to the boil. Add the apricots, bring back to a simmer and cook gently for 1–2 minutes, then remove the pan from the heat and set aside to cool.

Once cooled, transfer the apricots with their syrup to a bowl, cover with cling film and place in the fridge.

A few hours before serving, drain the apricots well in a sieve set over a pan, to catch the syrup. Place the pan over a medium heat, bring to the boil and let bubble to reduce by about one-quarter, then pour into a bowl. Leave to cool, then cover and refrigerate.

Put the mascarpone into another bowl and work it with a wooden spoon, to soften. If using a vanilla pod, split the pod lengthways in half and scrape out the seeds into the mascarpone, using the back of a small knife. Mix well, to distribute the vanilla seeds evenly. If using vanilla extract, simply mix it into the mascarpone.

Transfer the vanilla mascarpone to a piping bag fitted with a 1cm plain nozzle and pipe the mixture generously inside each apricot to fill it. (Alternatively, you can use a teaspoon.)

Arrange the stuffed apricots side by side in a shallow dish, cover loosely with cling film and chill in the fridge for an hour or two before serving.

To serve, spoon some of the chilled syrup over and around the apricots and scatter the chopped pistachios over the top. Serve the rest of the syrup in a small jug for guests to help themselves.

Ricotta with berries and passion fruit

400g mixed berries, such as red and yellow raspberries, redcurrants, blackberries, blueberries

1 small kiwi fruit (optional)

2 passion fruit

320g ricotta

80g demerara sugar

100ml double cream, to serve

This is a lovely, simple dessert to serve at the height of the summer when berries and fresh currants are at their seasonal best. Other fresh cheeses – goat's, cow's or ewe's – can be substituted for the ricotta, as long as they have a mild flavour and a semi-firm consistency. For a more savoury note, mix a few fine herbs, such as snipped chives or tarragon, into the cheese and season with a touch of salt and pepper, omitting the sugar topping.

Prepare the berries, removing any stems. Peel and slice the kiwi fruit, if using. Cut the passion fruit in half and use a teaspoon to scoop out the insides into a cup; set aside.

Place a plain pastry cutter, about 8cm in diameter and 3cm tall, in the middle of a chilled serving plate. Using a spoon, fill the ring with one-quarter of the ricotta, packing it in lightly. Lift off the ring, twisting it slightly as you lift, so that the ricotta keeps its shape. Repeat this process to shape the ricotta on the other 3 plates.

Dust the sugar evenly over the surface of each ricotta. Wave a cook's blowtorch over the top to partially melt and caramelise the sugar, as you would for a crème brûlée.

Distribute the berries, and kiwi fruit, if using, around each ricotta mound, and spoon the passion fruit juice and seeds over the fruit. Serve at once, with the cream in a jug on the side.

Filo-wrapped feta and griddled watermelon

SERVES 4

8 tbsp clear, runny honey

3 tbsp black sesame seeds

8 batons of feta, about 6cm long and 1cm wide

8 squares of filo pastry, 9 x 9cm

50ml light olive oil, for brushing

750ml grapeseed oil, for deep-frying

8 pinches of soft brown sugar

8 rectangles of ripe watermelon (ideally seedless), 4 x 2cm and 1cm thick, chilled

1–2 tsp white wine vinegar

Watermelon and feta are often brought together to make a refreshing savoury salad, but the combination also works beautifully as a dessert. This original recipe is appetising and easy to make. Take care as you bite into the filo parcels, as the soft feta inside may still be very hot.

Warm the honey gently. Sprinkle the sesame seeds into a very hot, dry frying pan and toast for 1 minute, then mix with the honey in a bowl. Spoon into 4 saucers or small dishes and set aside.

Thread each baton of feta lengthways onto a wooden skewer, taking care not to break it, and leaving 1–2cm of skewer free at one end.

Lay the filo squares on a work surface and brush them very lightly with olive oil. Place a feta skewer on one side of each filo square, then turn to wrap it up and enclose in the pastry, making sure the skewer is left exposed at one end. Set aside on a plate.

Heat the grapeseed oil in a deep-fryer or other large, heavy-based pan. Meanwhile, place a ridged griddle pan over a high heat. As soon as the oil reaches 160°C, add the wrapped feta batons and deep-fry for 1–2 minutes until the filo is a nice nut-brown colour. Remove and drain on kitchen paper.

Sprinkle the brown sugar evenly over the watermelon rectangles and place on the hot griddle pan. Cook for about 45 seconds, giving them a quarter-turn halfway through, to mark very lightly with a cross-hatch pattern. Turn and repeat on the other side, then transfer to a plate.

To serve, arrange a pair of filo-wrapped feta batons and a couple of griddled watermelon pieces on each warmed plate. Add a few drops of wine vinegar to each saucer of honey and sesame seed mixture and offer one to each guest, so that they can spoon it onto their feta batons – or dip them into it – as they go.

Coffee and mascarpone crème brûlée

SERVES 6

250ml milk

250g mascarpone

65g caster sugar

50g roasted coffee beans, finely crushed, plus 6 whole beans

4 egg yolks

30g demerara sugar

6 mint sprigs (optional)

Using mascarpone in place of the usual cream, these are decadent and very easy to prepare. If you do not have a cook's blowtorch, do invest in one – to create the classic crèmes brûlée caramel topping. Most kitchen shops and stores with a good cookware department now stock them.

In a small pan over a gentle heat, slowly heat the milk, mascarpone and 15g of the caster sugar, stirring from time to time with a small balloon whisk. As soon as it comes to the boil, remove from the heat and add the crushed coffee beans. Mix well, then cover the pan with cling film and set aside to infuse and cool slightly.

Using a small balloon whisk, mix the egg yolks with the remaining 50g caster sugar in a small bowl, then whisk well until it reaches a light, almost airy, ribbon consistency.

When the milk and mascarpone mixture has cooled to about 80°C, fold it gently into the egg yolk mixture. Set aside to cool, stirring with a spatula from time to time. Once cooled, cover with cling film and chill in the fridge for at least 12 hours.

To cook the crèmes, preheat the oven to 95°C/Gas lowest setting.

Place 6 crème brûlée moulds, about 11cm across the top, 9cm at the base and 2.5cm deep, on a baking sheet. Strain the chilled mixture through a fine chinois into a jug and pour it evenly into the moulds. Place in the oven and cook for 25 minutes.

Remove from the oven, leave to cool, then chill in the fridge for at least a couple of hours.

To finish, stand the crèmes brûlée dishes on your work surface and sprinkle a fine layer of demerara sugar evenly on top of each. Wave a cook's blowtorch over the surface to melt the sugar and create a fine layer of light caramel.

Stand each crème brûlée dish on a plate and place a whole coffee bean on top. Finish with a mint sprig, if you like.

Alsace fromage blanc tart

SERVES 6–8

350g flan pastry (see page 249)

Plain flour, for dusting

Butter, for greasing

For the filling

200g fromage blanc, 20–40% fat content (see below)

100g caster sugar, plus a pinch for the egg whites

300ml milk

6 medium eggs, separated

60g cornflour

Finely grated zest and juice of 1 lemon

It isn't easy to find fromage blanc, but as an alternative, you can use a combination of 140g quark and 60g full-fat Greek-style yoghurt.

This tart is as easy to make as it is to eat, and is particularly good served with a red fruit coulis. I sometimes flavour the filling with vanilla extract or a few drops of orange flower water rather than lemon. You can make this tart using a *pâte sablée* pastry case, but I much prefer *pâte à foncer* or flan pastry, which is still buttery and short but much less sweet, and complements the fromage blanc filling nicely.

Roll out the pastry on a lightly floured work surface to a circle, about 2mm thick and 32–34cm in diameter. Lightly butter a 22cm tart ring, 4–5cm deep, and place on a baking sheet. Loosely wrap the pastry around the rolling pin and unfurl it gently over the tart ring, making sure it keeps its shape. Press the pastry against the side of the ring and chill in the fridge for at least 20 minutes.

Meanwhile, preheat the oven to 180°C/Gas 4.

For the filling, put the fromage blanc, caster sugar, milk, egg yolks, cornflour and lemon zest and juice into a bowl and mix well with a balloon whisk until the mixture is completely homogeneous, without overworking it.

In a scrupulously clean and cold bowl, whisk the egg whites until stiff, adding the pinch of sugar once they are almost stiff. Using a spatula, gently fold the whipped egg whites into the egg yolk and fromage blanc mixture.

Pour the mixture into the chilled pastry case, filling it to the brim. Bake in the oven for 20 minutes, then lower the oven setting to 150°C/Gas 2 and cook for another 20 minutes.

Remove the tart from the oven and leave it in the ring for 5 minutes, then invert a baking tray lined with baking parchment over the ring and turn the tart upside down onto it, taking care not to burn yourself. Leave the tart upside down for 10 minutes, then carefully remove the tart ring by rotating it slightly.

Place a serving plate over the base of the tart and carefully turn it over again. The tart is best served once it has cooled slightly – either warm or at room temperature but definitely not chilled.

Orange cheesecake with honey and pistachios

SERVES 8–10

A baked cheesecake is always popular and the orange and pistachios give this one a delightful twist. The cheesecake will keep very well for several days in the fridge, without the final honey, orange zest and pistachio layer, which is added just before serving. (Illustrated on previous pages.)

For the base

Softened butter, for greasing

325g Digestive biscuits

90g butter, melted and cooled

For the filling and topping

3 oranges

250g caster sugar

100ml water

350g cream cheese, softened

350g curd cheese, softened

150ml soured cream

4 medium eggs

120g clear, runny honey

30g shelled, skinless pistachios

Very lightly grease the base and sides of a springform cake tin, 22–24cm diameter and 5–6cm deep, with softened butter and stand the tin on a baking sheet. Preheat the oven to 175°C/Gas 3½.

For the base, crush the biscuits to fine crumbs in a food processor, or place in a strong plastic bag and bash with a rolling pin. In a bowl, mix the crushed biscuits with the melted butter until fully combined.

Tip the biscuit crumb mixture into the prepared tin and spread it out to form an even layer, pressing it firmly and uniformly with your flattened knuckles. Bake in the oven for 12 minutes until the base has firmed up, like a pastry layer. Set aside, still on the baking sheet, and lower the oven setting to 140°C/Gas 1.

Using a swivel peeler, finely pare the zest of one of the oranges, removing it in strips, then cut these into long, thin julienne.

In a small pan, dissolve 75g of the sugar in the water over a medium heat and then bring to the boil. Add the orange zest julienne, reduce the heat to a simmer and poach the zest in the syrup for 10 minutes. Remove from the heat and leave to cool completely. Once cooled, drain the zest julienne.

Rub the skins of the remaining 2 oranges against the finest grating surface of a box grater to produce a wet zest purée. Scrape into a small bowl and set aside.

Cut all 3 oranges in half and squeeze to extract the juice, then strain through a fine chinois or sieve.

Cooling the cheesecake very slowly in the switched-off oven helps to prevent the surface from cracking. The filling will continue to firm up as it cools.

Put the cream cheese, curd cheese, soured cream and remaining 175g caster sugar into a large bowl and mix together well, until smoothly combined.

In another bowl, whisk the eggs until light and foamy, then strain through a fine chinois or sieve into the cream cheese mixture. Mix well with a wooden spoon, then add the orange juice and the orange zest purée and mix to combine.

Pour the mixture on top of the base in the tin and bake in the oven for 1½ hours. Turn off the oven and leave the cheesecake inside for another hour, with the door very slightly open.

Remove the cheesecake from the oven and leave to cool completely. Once cooled, refrigerate for at least 2–3 hours before serving.

When ready to serve, run a knife around the inside of the tin and gently release the side of the tin, then carefully transfer the cheesecake to a serving plate.

Using a palette knife, spread the honey over the surface of the cheesecake. Sprinkle a little of the candied orange zest julienne over the top, then scatter over the pistachios. To cut, use a very sharp knife – dipped in hot water in between cutting each slice.

Apple strudel with Pecorino

SERVES 4

For the pastry

3 sheets of filo pastry, about 55 x 20cm

60g clarified butter

For the filling

30g fine breadcrumbs

30g ground almonds

2 Braeburn or Cox apples (not too ripe), washed and dried

Juice of 1 lemon

60g soft brown sugar

1 tsp ground cinnamon

100g sultanas, blanched for 1 minute, refreshed, drained and patted dry

120g Pecorino Romano, cut into fine slivers, plus extra (optional) to serve

To finish

30g icing sugar, for dusting

Whipping cream, lightly whipped (optional)

This light, crisp strudel is full of flavour, the cheese marrying beautifully with the apples, spice and sultanas. You can, if you wish, use another semi-hard cheese in place of the Pecorino, provided the flavour is not too strong.

Preheat the oven to 180°C/Gas 4. Spread the breadcrumbs and ground almonds out on a baking tray and lightly toast in the oven for 3 minutes. Tip into a bowl, mix together and set aside.

Cut the apples in half and remove the core, then cut each half into fine slices, about 2mm thick. Put into a bowl with the lemon juice, sugar, ground cinnamon and sultanas. Mix gently, cover with cling film and set aside for 5 minutes.

Place one sheet of filo pastry on a clean tea towel, with the short side facing you. Very lightly brush the filo all over with clarified butter, then place a second sheet of filo on top, without pressing it down. Repeat with the third sheet.

Spread the apple and sultana mixture evenly over the filo, keeping a clear 3cm margin on all 4 sides. Sprinkle the breadcrumb and ground almond mixture evenly over the apples. Arrange the slivers of Pecorino here and there on top.

Line a large baking sheet with lightly buttered baking parchment. Now, with the aid of the tea towel and starting with the short side facing you, roll up the filo to enclose the filling and form a fat sausage shape, pressing lightly as you roll.

Place the strudel on the prepared baking sheet and bake for 25–30 minutes until crisp and golden. Using a large palette knife, immediately transfer to a wire rack and leave to cool a little, for 5–10 minutes.

Generously dust the top of the strudel with icing sugar, then slide onto a board or oblong serving plate. Cut into slices, using a sharp, serrated knife, and serve with whipped cream on the side, if you like, and maybe a few extra slices of Pecorino.

Apple tart with cheese shavings

SERVES 4

150ml milk

½ vanilla pod, split lengthways, or ½ tsp vanilla extract

1 medium egg

70g caster sugar

320g quick puff pastry (see page 249)

20g plain flour, plus extra for dusting

4 medium apples (not too ripe), preferably Cox or Gala

160g Prairie Breeze or fine-quality mature Cheddar

The idea of matching the superb American cheese Prairie Breeze with an apple tart was passed on to me by my colleague and friend Patrick O'Connell. A fine-quality, 12-month-aged Cheddar would be the best alternative.

Put the milk and vanilla into a pan and slowly bring to the boil over a low heat. Meanwhile, in a small bowl, mix the egg with 40g of the sugar, using a balloon whisk, then add the flour and mix again with the whisk until smoothly combined. Pour on the hot milk, stirring constantly with the whisk, then pour back into the pan and cook, stirring, over a low heat for 2 minutes.

Pour the mixture into a small bowl. Remove the vanilla pod and, using the back of a small knife, scrape out the seeds and return them to the mixture; discard the pod. If using vanilla extract, stir it in at this stage. Cover with cling film and set aside to cool.

Divide the pastry into 4 equal portions. On a lightly floured surface, roll out one portion of pastry to a circle, about 14cm in diameter and 2mm thick, and place on a baking tray. Repeat with the other 3 portions of pastry to make 4 bases. Place the tray in the fridge for at least 20 minutes to rest the pastry.

Meanwhile, preheat the oven to 200°C/Gas 6. Peel, halve and core the apples, then cut into fine slices, so you have a couple of sliced halves per tart.

Make sure the tart bases are perfectly round; if necessary, trim any excess using a small knife. Prick each base with a fork 10–12 times.

Divide the cooled custard mixture between the tart bases and spread it out evenly. Arrange the apple slices in a rosette on top, starting from the outside and working inwards towards the middle, overlapping the slices as you go. Sprinkle with the remaining sugar and bake for 25 minutes.

Remove from the oven and immediately transfer the tarts to a wire rack, using a palette knife. Leave to stand for a few minutes. To serve, place the just-warm tarts on individual plates, then arrange 4 or 5 slivers of cheese on top of each one. Serve with an extra few slivers of cheese on the side, if you like.

Ricotta cassata

Serves 8

2 freshly baked genoise sponges, 18.5cm in diameter and 4.5cm high (see page 250)

600g good-quality mixed glacé fruits of choice, such as mandarin, angelica, melon slices, orange peel, red and green cherries, etc.

60g dark chocolate couverture (ideally Valrhona)

100g caster sugar

600g ricotta, preferably cow's milk ricotta

150g marzipan

A few drops of green food colouring

For the syrup

50g caster sugar

30ml cold water

To finish

Icing sugar, sifted, for dusting

You only need the outside edge of the second genoise, you can save the unused sponge for teatime, serving it with a little jam.

This very sweet, creamy dessert of Sicilian origin is usually served at Easter. There are various different versions and I sometimes add a hint of orange flower water to the ricotta, which adds a delightful flavour. Creating the decorative sponge and marzipan border is a little fiddly, but it results in a stunning finish.

Using a serrated knife, slice one of the genoise sponges horizontally into 3 discs, each 1.5cm thick. Set aside one of the discs until ready to finish the cassata. Place the base disc on a plate.

Cut 150g of the least attractive glacé fruits into dice. Finely chop the chocolate. Mix the caster sugar with the ricotta, using a spatula, then mix in the diced glacé fruit and chopped chocolate.

Using the spatula, spread half the ricotta and fruit mixture over the genoise sponge base, then place the second disc on top, pressing down on it lightly with your fingertips so that it adheres evenly. Spread the remaining ricotta and fruit mixture evenly over the top. Cover with cling film and place in the fridge until ready to add the final layer of sponge.

Meanwhile, for the syrup, dissolve the sugar in the water in a small pan over a medium heat and let bubble for a minute until thickened and syrupy. Remove from the heat and set aside to cool.

Place the marzipan on a work surface and sprinkle with the green food colouring. Work it in, using the palm of your hand, until the marzipan is a uniform, very pale green colour. Wrap in cling film and place in the fridge.

Take the second genoise sponge and, using a serrated knife, cut thin slices, about 3mm thick, from around the edge, so that they are about 2cm across the base, and slightly wider at the top (due to the sloping sides). Trim these slices into symmetrical, tall trapezium shapes (or triangles with the point cut off).

continued overleaf

continued from previous page

On a very clean, dry work surface, roll out the green marzipan, dusting it a little with the icing sugar to prevent it from sticking to the rolling pin. Using a large chef's knife, cut trapezium shapes from the rolled-out marzipan, to the same dimensions as the sponge ones.

Take the cassata out of the fridge. Brush a little of the cooled syrup over the inside (sponge side) of a genoise trapezium, then stick this onto the side of the cassata. Do the same with a marzipan trapezium, placing it upside down and next to the sponge, so that it fits neatly. Continue in this way until the outside of the cassata is completely covered and evenly patterned.

Add the top disc of genoise sponge, cut side down, pressing it down lightly with your fingertips. Cover with cling film and set aside in the fridge until ready to serve.

To serve, place the cassata on a cake stand if you have one, to show it off to maximum effect. Dust the surface with just a little icing sugar, then arrange the remaining glacé fruits on top of the sponge. Your work of art is now ready to present to your guests.

Basics

Chicken stock

This stock has many uses in the kitchen. It should be skimmed from time to time. This is best carried out with a spoon or small skimmer, in order to remove any impurities and fats floating on the surface of the liquid.

MAKES ABOUT 1.5 LITRES

1 boiling fowl, weighing 1.5kg, or an equal weight of raw chicken carcasses or wings, blanched and refreshed

2.5 litres cold water

200g carrots, cut into chunks

2 leeks (white part only), well washed and cut into chunks

1 celery stalk, coarsely chopped

1 onion, studded with 2 cloves

150g button mushrooms, thinly sliced

1 bouquet garni

Put the chicken or carcasses into a large saucepan and pour on the cold water to cover. Bring to the boil over a high heat, then immediately lower the heat and keep at a simmer.

After 5 minutes, skim the surface and add all the other ingredients. Cook gently for 1½ hours, without boiling, skimming whenever necessary.

Strain the stock through a fine chinois into a bowl and cool over ice. Refrigerate and use within 4 or 5 days, or freeze for up to 3 months.

Fish stock

Cooking a stock for longer than suggested in the recipe does not make it better – quite the reverse. With lengthy cooking, a stock becomes heavy and loses its flavour; this applies particularly to fish stocks, which can also acquire a bitter taint.

MAKES 2 LITRES

1.5kg white fish bones and trimmings (from sole, turbot, brill, whiting, etc.), cut into pieces

50g butter

2 leeks (white part only), well washed and thinly sliced

75g onions, thinly sliced

75g button mushrooms, thinly sliced

200ml dry white wine

2.5 litres cold water

1 bouquet garni

2 lemon slices

8 white peppercorns, crushed and tied in muslin

Rinse the fish bones and trimmings under cold running water, then drain.

Melt the butter in a large saucepan, add the sliced vegetables and sweat gently over a low heat for a few minutes.

Add the fish bones and trimmings and allow to bubble gently for a few moments, then pour in the white wine. Cook until it has reduced by two-thirds, then add the cold water. Bring to the boil, then lower the heat, skim the surface and add the bouquet garni and lemon slices.

Simmer very gently for 25 minutes, skimming as necessary. About 10 minutes before the end of cooking, add the muslin-wrapped peppercorns.

Gently ladle the stock through a fine chinois into a bowl and cool over ice. Refrigerate and use within 2 or 3 days, or freeze for up to 3 months.

Vegetable stock

You can vary the ingredients for this stock according the season, adding a few flavourful, ripe tomatoes in summer, or a handful of wild mushrooms in the autumn, for example.

MAKES 1.5 LITRES

300g carrots, cut into rounds

2 leeks (white part only), well washed and thinly sliced

100g celery stalks, thinly sliced

50g fennel bulb, very thinly sliced

150g shallots, thinly sliced

100g onion, thinly sliced

2 unpeeled garlic cloves

1 bouquet garni

250ml dry white wine

2 litres cold water

10 white peppercorns, crushed and tied in muslin

Put all the ingredients, except the peppercorns, into a saucepan and bring to the boil over a high heat. Lower the heat and cook at a bare simmer for 45 minutes, skimming as necessary and adding the muslin-wrapped peppercorns after 35 minutes.

Strain through a fine chinois into a bowl and cool over ice. Refrigerate and use within 4 or 5 days, or freeze for up to 3 months.

Roquefort butter

This flavoured butter is exceptionally good on top of grilled or pan-fried steaks.

MAKES 250G

150g butter, softened

100g Roquefort

Freshly ground pepper

Put the softened butter into a bowl. Crumble in the Roquefort and work into the butter with a wooden spoon to combine. Briefly blitz in a blender until smooth or rub through a drum sieve with a plastic scraper. Season with pepper to taste.

Lay a sheet of cling film on your work surface and spoon the butter into the middle. Roll the butter in the cling film into a cylinder shape, about 5cm in diameter, twist the ends to seal and refrigerate or freeze until needed.

Unwrap the butter and cut into discs to use.

Béchamel sauce

Béchamel sauce is used in a variety of dishes, including cauliflower cheese (see page 186) and a classic croque-monsieur (see page 71). It also forms the basis of many other sauces. The sauce will keep in an airtight container in the fridge for up to 4 days; reheat in a bain-marie to serve.

MAKES 500ML

30g butter

30g plain flour

500ml cold milk

Freshly grated nutmeg (optional)

Sea salt and freshly ground white pepper

Melt the butter in a small, heavy-based saucepan over a low heat, then add the flour. Stir with a whisk and cook gently for 2–3 minutes to make a roux.

Pour the cold milk on to the roux, whisking as you do so, and bring to the boil over a medium heat, whisking continuously. When the sauce comes to the boil, lower the heat and simmer gently for about 10 minutes, stirring frequently. Season to taste with salt, white pepper and a little nutmeg if you wish, then pass the sauce through a fine chinois.

Either serve the béchamel sauce immediately or, if necessary, keep it warm in a bain-marie, dotting a few flakes of butter over the surface to stop a skin from forming.

Mornay sauce

You can coat poached eggs, vegetables, fish or white meats with this sauce, then lightly brown them under a hot grill. Or mix with macaroni to make a classic macaroni cheese. The sauce will keep in an airtight container in the fridge for a couple of days; reheat in a bain-marie to serve.

SERVES 4–6

30g butter

30g plain flour

500ml cold milk

A pinch of freshly grated nutmeg (optional)

3 egg yolks

50ml double cream

100g Gruyère, Emmenthal or Cheddar, finely grated

Sea salt and freshly ground white pepper

First make a béchamel. Melt the butter in a small, heavy-based saucepan over a low heat, then add the flour. Stir with a whisk and cook gently for 2–3 minutes to make a white roux.

Pour the cold milk on to the roux, whisking as you do so, and bring to the boil over a medium heat, whisking constantly. When the sauce comes to the boil, lower the heat and simmer gently for about 10 minutes, stirring frequently. Season to taste with nutmeg, salt and white pepper.

Mix the egg yolks and double cream together in a bowl, then pour the mixture into the béchamel, whisking all the time. Let the sauce bubble for about 1 minute, whisking continuously, then take the pan off the heat and shower in the grated cheese. Stir until melted, then taste and adjust the seasoning if necessary.

Either serve immediately or, if necessary, keep the sauce warm in a bain-marie, dotting a few flakes of butter over the surface to stop a skin from forming.

Barbecue sauce

I love this sauce, especially served with my tacos (see page 67), or with burgers topped with a slice of melted lightly smoked cheese. It's also very good for dipping fried chicken wings into.

SERVES 8–10

30ml light olive oil

125g onions, chopped

10g garlic, chopped

25g fresh ginger, cut into fine slices

60g runny honey

50ml white wine vinegar

100g tomato purée

100g tomato ketchup

30ml Worcestershire sauce

10g English mustard powder

250ml chicken stock (see page 244 for home-made)

Sea salt and freshly ground pepper

Heat the olive oil in a medium saucepan over a low heat, then add the onions, garlic and ginger and cook until softened and golden, stirring from time to time.

Add the honey, increase the heat slightly and cook until the onions are lightly caramelised, then add the wine vinegar, stirring to deglaze. Stir in the tomato purée and simmer for 2–3 minutes, then add the remaining ingredients, except salt and pepper, and bring to the boil. Reduce the heat to low and leave to simmer for 35–40 minutes, skimming the surface every 5–10 minutes.

Strain the mixture through a chinois into a bowl, pressing lightly with the back of a small ladle to extract all the flavours. Season with salt and pepper to taste and set aside to cool. Store in the fridge, covered with cling film, until ready to use.

Pistou

Pistou adds a Mediterranean flourish to a finished dish, particularly pasta dishes. I use it in many recipes, including my tomato and burrata salad (page 86) and cauliflower gratin (see page 186). Pistou keeps for at least 2 weeks in the fridge, or longer if you're not constantly taking it in and out.

MAKES ABOUT 220G

5g garlic, halved, green germ removed (if present) and crushed with the flat of a knife

50g pine nuts

75g basil leaves

75g Parmesan, freshly grated

300ml olive oil

Sea salt and freshly ground pepper

Put the garlic, pine nuts and a pinch of salt into a food processor and blitz for 30 seconds. Add the basil and process for another 30 seconds, then add the Parmesan and blitz again for 30 seconds. Using a spatula, bring any mixture or ingredients sticking to the sides into the middle and blitz briefly to combine.

With the machine on a low speed, pour in the olive oil in a thin stream, as you would for mayonnaise, until all the oil has been absorbed. Season generously with pepper and transfer the pistou to a jar with a lid. Keep in the fridge until ready to use.

Green olive tapenade

I often pair tapenade with fresh goat's cheese (see page 36). I also use it in little puff pastry tourtes, mingled with young sheep or goat's cheese and semi-confit tomatoes (page 185). I don't like to overwork the olives because they lose a little of their colour – that's why I chop them with a knife, as I do for the other ingredients, before adding them to the processor and blitzing briefly.

MAKES ABOUT 360G

200g green olives, pitted and roughly chopped

60g anchovy fillets (pliable and not overly salty), diced

2 medium garlic cloves, green germ removed (if present) and crushed with the flat of a knife

30g capers, drained and chopped

100ml light but fruity olive oil

Juice of ½ lemon, or to taste (optional)

Sea salt and freshly ground pepper

Put all the ingredients except the olive oil, lemon juice and seasoning into a food processor. Process for 30–45 seconds then, on a low speed, slowly pour in the olive oil in a thin stream, as you would for mayonnaise. Once the mixture is homogeneous (after about a minute), add a little salt and a generous grinding of pepper, then finally add the lemon juice, if using.

Transfer the tapenade to a jar with a lid and keep it in the fridge until ready to use. You will need to give the tapenade a stir each time you use it, to ensure it is homogeneous. It keeps very well in the fridge for 8–10 days.

Black olive tapenade

Substitute black olives for green, reduce the quantity of anchovy fillets to 20g and omit the salt.

Semi-confit cherry tomatoes

I use these semi-confit tomatoes in several recipes, including Parmesan lace shells (see page 24), lobster gratin (see page 111) and confit of pork belly (see page 150). They add a welcome touch of colour, sweetness and freshness. The oil can be kept for a few days and used in dressings or other recipes.

MAKES 10–14 CHERRY TOMATOES

200ml light olive oil

1 thyme sprig

1 bay leaf

½ garlic clove, peeled

10–14 cherry tomatoes

Heat the olive oil in a saucepan over a medium heat to about 90°C and add the thyme, bay leaf, garlic and cherry tomatoes. Lower the heat and confit at about 70°C until the tomato skins are just starting to show signs of splitting – about 8–10 minutes, depending on size and ripeness. Remove the pan from the heat and set aside to cool.

Transfer the tomatoes to a jar or bowl, and pour over the oil. Cover and refrigerate until ready to use. The semi-confit tomatoes will keep well in their oil in the fridge for a couple of weeks.

Flan pastry

This pastry has a lovely crispness and is fairly easy to work with. It can be kept in the fridge for a week or in the freezer for up to 3 months. Leave out the sugar if you are making a savoury tart.

MAKES ABOUT 400G

250g plain flour

125g butter, cut into small pieces and slightly softened

1 medium egg

1 tsp caster sugar (optional)

½ tsp fine sea salt

40ml cold water

Heap the flour on a clean work surface, make a well in the middle and add the butter, egg, sugar and salt. With your fingertips, mix and cream the ingredients in the well.

Now, little by little, draw the flour into the centre and work the dough with your fingertips to a grainy texture. Add the cold water and mix it in until the dough begins to hold together.

Using the palm of your hand, push the dough away from you 4 or 5 times until it is completely smooth. Roll the pastry into a ball, wrap in cling film and refrigerate until ready to use.

Quick puff pastry

This quick puff pastry rises well – almost 75% as much as classic puff pastry and is much quicker to make. Tightly wrapped in cling film, it will keep for 3 days in the fridge, and for at least 4 weeks in the freezer.

MAKES 1.2KG

500g plain flour, plus extra for dusting

500g very cold butter, cut into small cubes

1 tsp fine sea salt

250ml ice-cold water

Heap the flour in a mound on a clean work surface and make a well. Put in the butter and salt and work them together with the fingertips of one hand, gradually drawing the flour into the centre with the other hand.

When the cubes of butter have become small pieces and the dough is grainy, gradually add the iced water and mix until it is all incorporated, but don't overwork the dough. Roll it into a ball, wrap in cling film and refrigerate for 20 minutes.

Flour the work surface and roll out the pastry into a 40 x 20cm rectangle. Fold it into three and give it a quarter-turn. Roll the block of pastry into a 40 x 20cm rectangle as before, and fold it into three again. These are the first 2 turns. Wrap the block in cling film and refrigerate it for 30 minutes.

Give the chilled pastry another 2 turns, rolling and folding as before. This makes a total of 4 turns. Wrap the pastry in cling film and refrigerate for at least 30 minutes before using.

Choux pastry

Choux pastry forms the basis of gougères – the cheese-flavoured choux buns I love to serve as a canapé (see page 27). The pastry can be mildly sweet or savoury. For a savoury version, omit the sugar.

MAKES A 4-EGG QUANTITY

125ml milk

125ml water

100g butter, diced

½ tsp salt

1 tsp caster sugar

150g plain flour

4 medium eggs

Eggwash (1 egg yolk mixed with 1 tbsp milk)

Combine the milk, water, butter, salt and sugar in a saucepan and set over a low heat. Bring to the boil. Immediately take the pan off the heat and shower in the flour, mixing as you do so with a wooden spoon until completely smooth.

Return the pan to a medium heat and stir continuously for about 1 minute to dry out the paste, then tip it into a large bowl. Add the eggs one at a time, beating thoroughly with the wooden spoon between each addition.

Once the eggs are all incorporated, the paste should be smooth and shiny with a thick ribbon consistency. It is now ready to use. (If you're not using it immediately, brush the surface lightly with a little beaten egg to prevent a crust forming.)

Genoise

This classic, butter-enriched whisked sponge has many uses. It also freezes well.

MAKES A 20CM SPONGE CAKE

20g softened butter, for greasing

125g plain flour, plus extra for dusting

4 medium eggs, at room temperature

125g caster sugar

30g butter, melted and cooled to tepid

Preheat the oven to 190°C/Gas 5. Brush a 20cm cake tin lightly with the butter and dust with flour.

Put the eggs and sugar into a bowl and whisk together. Continue to whisk for about 12 minutes until the mixture is pale and thickened enough to leave a ribbon trail when you lift the whisk. (You can also do this in an electric mixer.)

Shower in the flour and delicately fold it into the mixture, with a rubber spatula. Add the melted butter and fold in carefully, without overworking the mixture. Pour the mixture into the cake tin.

Bake for 30 minutes or until it is cooked. To test, lightly press the centre of the sponge with your fingertips; there should be a slight resistance. Invert on to a wire rack, giving the sponge a quarter-turn after 10 minutes to prevent it sticking. Leave to cool for 3–4 hours.

Index

Dedication

I would like to dedicate this book to my wife Robyn, for her patience and encouragement, whether it has been in checking my text or in tasting my new recipes, wherever we happen to be in the world: Switzerland, France, Italy, etc.

Acknowledgements

Janet Illsley, who advised and guided me with utmost professionalism and good humour throughout this book's gestation.

Sally Somers, with whom it was a real pleasure to work, not only on the translations but also in detecting the odd misprint in my manuscript. She is a highly valued member of the team.

Claude Grant, who found a way to devote her limited free time to typing and editing my French manuscript. She is an absolute gem.

Lisa Linder, who built on her first joint endeavour with us, The Essence of French Cooking, to create another stunning success, with photographs that are both brilliant and unexpected.

Lucy Gowans, whose trained eye gave a huge boost to my energy and creativity levels. A big bravo!

Frankie Unsworth, whose choice of colours and shapes for fabrics and tableware were a delight, and so perfectly enhanced my illustrated recipes.

For the loan of special equipment for photography, I am grateful to Androuet and Staub.

In addition, Tefal have generously supplied me with their excellent non-stick pans and bakeware.

Finally, I would like to thank my chef friends who have been happy to share their knowledge of cheeses from their countries, in particular: Luke Mangan, who introduced me to Australian cheeses; Patrick O'Connell, who taught me much more about American cheeses; and Brian Turner, for his bounteous knowledge of English cheese.

Publishing director **Sarah Lavelle**
Creative director **Helen Lewis**
Project editor **Janet Illsley**
Design and art direction **Lucy Gowans**
Translator **Sally Somers**
Photographer **Lisa Linder**
Stylist **Frankie Unsworth**
Production **Tom Moore, Vincent Smith**

First published in 2017 by
Quadrille Publishing Limited
www.quadrille.co.uk

Text © 2017 Michel Roux
Photography © 2017 Lisa Linder
Design and layout © 2017 Quadrille
Publishing Limited
The rights of the author have been asserted.

Cataloguing in Publication Data:
a catalogue record for this book is available from the British Library.
ISBN 978 1 84949 966 8
Printed in China